SHY

Sian Prior is a journalist and broadcaster specialising in the arts and popular culture, a media consultant, and a teacher at universities and writers centres. She has a second career as a musician and recording artist. *Shy* is her first book.
sianprior.com

SHY

A MEMOIR

SIAN PRIOR

TEXT PUBLISHING MELBOURNE AUSTRALIA

textpublishing.com.au

The Text Publishing Company
Swann House
22 William Street
Melbourne Victoria 3000 Australia

First published by The Text Publishing Company 2014
Reprinted 2014

Cover design by W. H. Chong
Page design and typesetting by Imogen Stubbs

Printed in Australia by Griffin Press, an Accredited ISO AS/NZS 14001:2004 Environmental Management System printer.

National Library of Australia Cataloguing-in-Publication entry (pbk)
Author: Prior, Sian, author.
Title: Shy : a memoir / by Sian Prior.
ISBN: 9781922182272 (paperback)
ISBN: 9781925095258 (ebook)
Subjects: Prior, Sian. Social phobia. Bashfulness.
             Emotions. Women authors—Biography.
Dewey Number: 155.232

This book is printed on paper certified against the Forest Stewardship Council® Standards. Griffin Press holds FSC chain-of-custody certification SGS-COC-005088. FSC promotes environmentally responsible, socially beneficial and economically viable management of the world's forests.

'I don't require changes from the surf, now diligent, now sluggish, obeying not me...'
Wisława Szymborska, 'Parting With A View', *Poems New and Collected*

CONTENTS

PART ONE

PART ONE

Prologue

Twice in the past thirty years I have extracted a mirror from my bedroom. The second time, not so long ago but in a different life, I returned with a screwdriver in my pocket to the house I had shared with Tom. After making sure that he wasn't home I slipped inside and knelt in front of the wardrobe beside our bed, the screwdriver threatening to escape from my shaking hands. A few twists for each screw; I loosened the metal brackets and gently lifted the glass from the front of the wardrobe door. The blue reflection of the bedspread disappeared, replaced by my own headless torso as I carried the mirror out onto the verandah, across the overgrown lawn, through the gate and onto the footpath, head down to avoid the gaze of any curious neighbours. I laid the mirror on a blanket in the back of my car and drove home to my sister's house.

I have been learning a lot about fear lately. It comes in many guises and one of the strangest is *catoptrophobia*: the fear of mirrors. Or, more accurately, the fear of the reflections within mirrors. Some catoptrophobics are afraid of their own image in the mirror. Some are afraid of words that are reflected by mirrors. Others fear that a mirror might steal their soul.

I wonder if there's a different term to describe a fear of the reflections to be found in mirrors that no longer reflect you.

But Why?

That's not where it began.

It began a couple of years earlier. At a birthday party. It began with me standing outside of me, watching as I stood silently on the fringe of a group of strangers. A familiar sensation was seeping through my body. It was as if someone had spiked my drink so that instead of sparkling mineral water I was now sipping a kind of effervescent cement. My limbs were growing rigid and my smile was the tight rictus you see on the faces of young ballet dancers.

The birthday girl was busy talking to other people and I couldn't see anyone else I recognised. My partner Tom was there, somewhere, in that art gallery full of strangers. Tom's football team had triumphed and he had celebrated with a couple of whiskies between leaving the ground and meeting me at the party. Now I couldn't find him in the crowd.

Sweat was trickling down the insides of my arms under a green jumper that felt too tight and no doubt looked too bright.

My stomach was churning and my fingers gripped the glass so hard they were beginning to ache. And now I was watching myself sidling towards the door.

The car needs to be moved. A one hour park won't be enough. There must be a better one somewhere close by. Or far away. At home, perhaps.

My movements had become as fluid as a cat after a bird. Putting down my glass of fizzy concrete, I moved three steps closer to the door, passing a wall mirror on the way. A calm, confident blonde woman in a perfectly fitting green jumper glanced back at me as I passed by.

A few seconds later I was outside and free and moving so fast it must have looked suspicious but I could see the car and I was pressing the blue button on the key ring and the headlights were flashing and my fingers had hold of the door handle and I was inside the car and alone and safe.

After a few deep breaths I started the engine and drove around the block, trying to decide what to do. An empty parking spot with no time limit soon appeared, so there went my one excuse for not returning to the party. Still, I couldn't go back.

I pulled over, found the phone and sent Tom a text, apologising for my disappearance and telling him I'd see him later. I couldn't remember when I had last felt this lonely.

I turned off the phone and restarted the car and drove slowly home. If it hadn't been so pathetic I would have laughed out loud. What was a polite middle-aged woman doing leaving a party without even saying goodbye to her partner, let alone the host?

Regressing, that's what. Behaving like she used to before she became Professional Sian. Like she did in the bad old days, when she was Shy Sian.

Shy. It's such a shy word; a timid little word that begs to remain unnoticed. Only three letters long and it begins with an exhortation to silence: '*shhh*'.

Reserved is something different. Tall men with jutting jaws. Prime ministers can be reserved, but never shy. And *quiet* implies choice; you *could* be loud but you prefer not to, instead perhaps watching purposefully, critically, from the sidelines. Strong, silent types are quiet. People like Tom.

Restrained carries itself with dignity, with an implication of control. Even *introvert* has a whiff of clinical authority about it. Myers and Briggs have awarded these people an impressive three-syllable label. And most introverts probably don't mind the label. They have proven themselves useful in the workplace; they make a positive contribution to group dynamics; they don't usually embarrass themselves in public.

But with the word shy there's no authority, no control. It's a blushing, hunching word; a nervous, knock-kneed, wallflower word. A word for children, not grown-ups, because surely grown-ups grow out of shyness. Don't they?

If I hadn't been so shy, I could have conducted a little research project at that birthday party. Pretended for a moment that I was a psychologist like my mother. Asked everyone else how they were feeling, probably found out that I was not the only guest with a burning desire to melt through the floorboards. If I had been pretending to be a psychologist in order to conduct my research project with the partygoers, I probably wouldn't have used the word shyness. Apparently the correct term for this thing is *social anxiety*, a term that has been leached of the redeeming sweetness of ye olde worlde shyness. Jane Austen's heroines could be shy but still lovable: young ladies of fine character, excellent marriage material.

A *socially anxious* person, on the other hand, is best avoided. Anxiety can be contagious, leaping from person to person like static electricity. I know because I've observed myself passing it along on countless occasions.

Social anxiety may lack the poetry of *shyness* but, once you put the symptoms together, it's hard to argue with the diagnosis. If you're feeling shy you're worried about something. If you're a persistent worrier, you're anxious. If you're anxious, your mind enters into a pact with your body, sending it forth into the world with an armoury of self-protective physical responses. Danger! The adrenaline, the sweating, the rapid breathing, all preparing your body to run. Ensuring your hands will shake but your legs will move faster when you need to take off.

Except that you're never sure why you needed to take off so fast in the first place.

Back home after the birthday party I gave myself, as always, a very hard time. Reformed alcoholics berate themselves every time they fall off the wagon; I'd spent a lifetime mentally beating myself up every time I gave in to my anxiety. What on earth was there to be afraid of? Why was I still dealing with this irrational response to the company of strangers? How would I explain my sudden disappearance to the birthday girl, and to Tom?

I tried to remember previous battles with better outcomes: parties that had started as Hieronymus Bosch triptychs and metamorphosed into Bruegel weddings, where I'd ended up swapping email addresses with half the guests. Alcohol had often helped, I remembered. But this time I was on the wagon in preparation for a singing recital—hence the mineral water. Did that put me in the clichéd category of grog-dependent social animals?

Waiting alone in bed for Tom to return, my self-flagellation changed shape. I was in my forties now. Too old to be sideswiped by these ridiculous fears. Too stubborn to let myself avoid situations that might provoke them. There had to be a way, at the very least, to control this thing.

And to control something, surely you must first understand it. As a journalist, I had made a living out of asking questions. Lying there in the dark under the blue bedspread, I began listing them in my mind.

What exactly *was* shyness and how did other shy people feel?
Was shyness really the same as introversion?
If so, how could I account for my complicated professional life, which had mostly involved being a show-off in front of a multitude of strangers? Showing off as a radio presenter, showing off in newspaper articles, showing off as a musician, showing off as a writing teacher, showing off so often that most people would never believe me if I told them I was shy.

Where had it come from, this fear?
Was shyness born or bred, or both?
Were there any advantages to being shy?
Did shyness ever magically disappear?
Why was I still fighting this battle after all these years?
And why did that matter so much to me?

One of my extroverted friends used to roll her eyes and say 'Shyness is SUCH a waste of time' and she was right. All the blushing, trembling and hyperventilating—or working hard not to blush, tremble and hyperventilate—chewed up an insane amount of emotional energy. I wondered whether there could possibly be any evolutionary benefit from such an affliction.

Affliction. What a word—almost biblical. The work of evil spirits acting on behalf of the Devil. We the afflicted must battle the malicious authors of these mysterious maladies in order to attain a state of grace.

In my family we held no truck with the Bible and its invisible agents of evil. In my family, mysteries were simply things about which you hadn't yet asked enough questions. And yet that state of grace, or at the very least equanimity in the presence of human company—that was something I had battled for. And the cause of my distress had remained a mystery.

What If?

When I was ten years old I had a friend called Sally who lived up the road and around the corner. She'd been to Disneyland.

Sally had sporty parents who always wore runners. They taught Physical Education at the local high school and were as short as each other. Sally's family had spent some time living in America (America! Where colours were brighter and everything happened long before it happened here, where everyone spoke televisionese and they had Disneyland in 3D). The sporty parents talked to us kids like we were adults and all the kids in Sally's family had blue eyes like all the people in America.

Sally was my best friend at primary school, when she could fit me in around also being best friends with the other Sally in our class whose dad went to Vietnam and then came home and killed himself and wasn't that a strange thing to have in common with someone, a dead dad? We all played netball at lunchtime and because I was tall I got to be goalkeeper and because Sally was small like her shorty sporty parents she played centre. And on the weekends when I was bored I would miss Sally and her neat, hard little netball throws and I wished we could play together.

'She's just up the road and round the corner,' my mum said. 'Why don't you go over there?'

Over there they had:

A basketball ring

A trampoline

Handsome brothers who could do tricks on the trampoline

Coca-Cola

A colour television

At home we had:

Fruit trees

A piano

A stepfather who sold trucks

A sister who was almost never home

A brother who played the trumpet

A lot of books

A framed picture of Bertrand Russell

'It's such a shame you won't go and visit Sally,' my mother said.

What if: I got there and Sally was busy playing with the other Sally and they didn't want me there?

What if: I got there and Sally was out and I'd have to make grown-up small talk with the shorty sporty moustachioed dad?

What if: I got there and the eldest blue-eyed brother looked at me and I blushed?

What if: I got there and Sally wasn't playing with anyone else but she said she was too busy to play with me?

What if: I got halfway there and decided Sally probably wouldn't want me there and I had to turn around and come home?

What if: I got there and Sally didn't want me there?

I could no more go up the road and around the corner than I could go to Disneyland.

Not long ago I sat in the conference room of a swanky city hotel and heard those two words *what if* repeated over and over. In my spare time I had begun trying to answer my list of shyness questions. A simple Google search had already turned up some useful information.

If asked, up to forty per cent of us would describe ourselves as shy. At least thirteen per cent of us spend some part of our lives suffering from a form of shyness so extreme that it has been labelled a phobia. But in my town, Google told me, there were 'recovery' programs available for sufferers, and the same organisation that offered those recovery programs also ran an annual seminar on social anxiety. I decided to check it out.

Calming ambient music wafted around us as we all took our seats in front of a wall of art deco mirrors. I wonder who thought seating a bunch of shy, self-conscious people in front of a bank of mirrors was a good idea? A female psychologist from the Anxiety Resource Centre walked to the lectern and began describing the typical thought processes of the socially anxious. 'Here's a case study,' she told us.

> She's a woman in her thirties and she's been working in the same small business for fifteen years. She did very well at school, well enough to enrol in a law course. So she drove to university for her first class. But she couldn't get out of the car. She was too afraid. 'What if the other students think I'm stupid, or awkward? What if the teacher thinks I'm weird?' she thought to herself. So she drove home again and instead of becoming a

lawyer she got a job in accounts, where she didn't have to interact with many people. She never applied for a promotion or took up any training opportunities in her job because that would involve putting herself forward. But she was bored and depressed working in accounts, she was actually highly intelligent, so ten years after her first attempt, she applied to do law again. Once again she was accepted and once again she drove to university for her first class. This time she managed to get out of the car and go to a tutorial. But she was extremely uncomfortable being surrounded by all those strangers. And when the teacher told everyone they would have to do a verbal presentation of an essay, she panicked. 'What if I open my mouth and I can't speak? What if the other students laugh at me? What if the teacher thinks I'm an idiot?' The woman fled the class and never returned.

And if I had been there too, that first time? If I had clambered off my stepfather's motor scooter in the university car park and noticed the woman sitting in her car, gripping the steering wheel as if she was on a ship in heavy seas? Would I have realised she was just like me, steeling herself against rising terror? Would I have knocked on the car window and offered her a shy smile?

Or if I had been there the second time? If I had sat next to her at the back of the crowded tutorial room, would I have seen her rigid shoulders, her shaking hands? Would we have recognised each other, felt the thrum of each other's anxiety, heard the silent whisper of each other's *what ifs*? Or would we have remained invisible to each other, both avoiding eye contact with everyone in the room, in case we were found out?

Would I have kept my head down but my ears open, listening out for the most talkative student, the one who made the grumpy tutor smile in spite of himself, nursing a small hope that this extrovert would notice me, take me under their wing, rescue me?

I'm afraid so.

If you're shy, the words *what if* line up in front of you like a row of hurdles on an athletics track. Leap over one and there's another one waiting for you. Some days it can be hard to find the energy to keep leaping.

My grandmother Peg Jones rarely encountered the *what if* hurdles. Or if she did, she hurtled towards them so fast she knocked them flying. Peg had no fear. She would talk to anyone, anywhere, about anything. Complete strangers would be bailed up and enlightened about her grandchildren's prodigious (and at times imaginary) talents. Teenagers nodding under headphones would be enlisted to carry her shopping trolley on and off buses. Random dog-walkers would be encouraged to help her pick up litter on the bay beach she loved.

And she would help anyone out, anytime, whether they needed it or not. Peg wasn't a Bible-basher, but she went to church often and she took her Christianity seriously. Her God had high expectations of her. She did her best to meet them. She picked up old ladies from nursing homes to do their supermarket shopping. She looked after the neighbours' triplets when the parents needed a break. She leafleted entire suburbs for the local politician she supported. And, perhaps in resolution of some simple karmic equation, when she asked for help it would usually be given.

As a child, I was often embarrassed by this free exchange of facts, fabrications and favours. 'What if they don't *want* to know that I play the clarinet?' I begged her. 'What if they don't *need* your help?' ('What if they think you're a crazy lady?' was one question I never spoke out loud, nor its anxious corollary, 'What if they think I'm crazy like you?') Peg would look at me as if I was speaking a foreign language and hurtle onwards.

As an adult I learned to admire this quality of fearlessness in Peg, even to envy it. I grew protective of her in these encounters, filling in the gaps for surprised strangers, like a translator. 'Peg's been looking after this beach for years,' I would explain. 'She helped plant these dune grasses herself. She really hates to see rubbish lying around.' Or 'Peg is nearly ninety, you know, she's very independent but she needs some help getting down the bus steps.'

And when, as an eighty-three-year-old widow, Peg fell breathlessly in love with a dapper gent a couple of years her senior, my admiration only grew. When she took the two single beds that she and my late grandfather Lloyd had occupied and converted them into a double bed for lovers, there were no *what if*s. (What if her friends are shocked? What if her daughters are offended? What if she breaches some unspoken rule about sex between octogenarians?)

When Peg and her boyfriend bought themselves a tandem bicycle and took to cycling up and down the beach path each morning with Peg's small dog perched in a basket on the handlebars, there were no *what if*s. (What if she falls off? What if he has a heart attack? What if people driving past in their cars laugh at these silver-haired eccentrics?) Peg just pedalled on into the bracing sea breeze.

Four grandparents: Peg and Lloyd, Mavis and Stan. And before them, eight great-grandparents. Sixteen great-great-grandparents. Ad infinitum. All that DNA, flowing like sap down the family tree. All those character traits pooling in a random puddle of personality. Where did Peg's fearlessness go? Such a strong streak in her character, so apparently absent in her blinking, blanching grand-daughter.

Perhaps not absent. Just trapped, like an insect in amber, by chronic embarrassment.

The Boys

I began borrowing books from the library. Books on blushing, on embarrassment, on anxiety. Journal articles about the parenting of shy children, about the distinction between shyness and introversion. They piled up on the bedside table, teetering towers of tomes with alliterative titles and ludicrously long subtitles.

Tom was reading the Bible again.

'But you don't believe in God anymore,' I said. 'You're lapsed. You don't think those stories are all true, do you? Surely it's just one big mash-up.'

'Who knows what's truth and what's fiction?' Tom answered. 'Does it matter? It's the poetry that interests me.'

I remember believing in Father Christmas.

I remember believing in the Tooth Fairy.

Clearly, as a child, I had no problem with magical thinking.

But I don't remember believing in God, which was a pity. An invisible friend would have come in handy when I was gripped by the *what if*s.

Once, though, I thought He was worth a try.

In grade five things were on the turn. Boys and girls had moved from occupying separate demarcated zones in the schoolyard to 'going round' with each other. Sally had an eleventh birthday party and invited some boys and she went into her bedroom and kissed one with her tongue and then she came out of her bedroom and told us all about it. She said he tasted of Twisties.

I felt sick.

I could almost taste those wet salty crumbs in my own mouth, feel his gluey tongue poking around my back teeth, imagine his orange saliva mingling with my fizzy lemonade spit. Sick.

But still. I wanted one of the boys to *want* to kiss me.

Boys didn't kiss shy girls, especially not tall, awkward, bookish ones. They barely even noticed us.

Then one day some magic happened.

On the walk home from school somehow I contrived to invite some boys to my house and—miracle of miracles—they came.

They came in a hurly-burly bunch of boyness, their grey school shirts streaked with darker patches of grey from falling over (boys were always falling over, they seemed to love it; I couldn't think of anything worse), their shoes smelly, their hair sweaty. They came down our driveway and into our backyard and there they discovered our orange tree, heavy with unripe fruit.

Oranges became missiles.

All the boys took turns picking green oranges from the tree and hurling them over the fence and into the neighbour's swimming pool. Every splash raised a cheer from the boys. (Boys were so loud.)

Mum was at work. My teenage sister Yoni was never home. Where was my brother David? I don't know. There was just the eruption of boys and the hard green missiles zinging through the air into the invisible swimming pool. And deep in the pit of my stomach the fizzy excitement of Having The Boys There mingled with the salty terror of What The Boys Were Doing and I wanted them to stay/go/please stay/please go/just go now/ would you all go away now please?

But I said nothing. Shyness had got my tongue.

Eventually, when all the green oranges were gone, all The Boys went home, leaving me to wait for The Repercussions.

And soon after my mother arrived home from work there was a knock on the front door and from the other end of the hallway I could tell it was the neighbour. And though I couldn't hear what was being said, from the apologetic pitch of my mother's voice I knew that now she knew. About The Boys.

Then she came to the room I shared with my brother and words were spoken and the ones I remember are: *You must go next door in the morning and apologise.*

Apologise to The Neighbour. An adult whom I didn't know but to whom I would have to make my shameful confession. About The Boys.

That's the first time I wanted to die.

And that's the last time I tried God.

I lay in bed that night hyperventilating with fear and having a silent word—the last word—with God.

If you do something that stops me having to go next door and apologise to The Neighbour, God, I said, *I will believe in you. I will. Always, from now on. If not, I would like to die now.*

It seemed like quite a good deal for God.

But He failed to deliver and that was it for me and God.

And, with the exception of one persistent redhead, that was it for me and The Boys for a long time.

They were too dangerous for shy girls.

Mistaken Identity

Cold air on the back of the neck. The smell of boiled cabbage and milk custard.

In a long lunch queue in an interminable lunch hour in a noisy cafeteria in an overcrowded comprehensive school in bus-clogged London at the fag end of the 1970s slouched a tall fourteen-year-old with a haircut she regretted.

A tap on the shoulder. Two pretty girls in blue pencil skirts. Both frowning. 'Excuse me, but we was just wondering, are you a boy or a girl?'

He/she/it stopped breathing.

Something shifted and crumbled. The last certainty. The thing I couldn't laugh at. 'Girl,' I whispered and turned away.

My mother Margot, a psychologist, had taken study leave from her academic job in Melbourne to spend six months at London's Maudsley Hospital. My sister Yoni had just finished high school and left home but the rest of our family—me, my brother David and our stepfather John—accompanied Margot to England.

There had been a few laughs, new-school tales recounted by my brother and me when we were safely back home in our green-carpeted rental flat in Dulwich. One of my classmates had inquired, 'How come you speak such good English?' *Neighbours* hadn't been invented yet; Londoners watched *Coronation Street*. Australia was a mutant starfish clinging to the other side of the spinning globe. *Terra nullius* for the schoolkids of Crystal Palace and Dulwich. My accent was, at times, impossible for them to understand.

'Are all Australians really tall like you and your brother?' was another question, and 'What are you hiding in that briefcase you carry around with you all the time?'

The 'briefcase' was a velvet-lined double clarinet case that I carted from class to class, waiting for after-school big band practice: the only time I felt anything close to comfortable among the other students. No speech required, just another piping tone in the mix of hoots and tweets and blasts. Sometimes when I arrived early for practice the West Indian boys who played in the steel drum band would be swaying in a ragged line, brown arms waving over the metal pans like card-trick magicians, conjuring the sound of shy church bells seduced by calypso. I wanted to curl up inside one of those drums and let the music undo me.

I can't remember whose idea the short haircut was. Maybe mine—a new me for a new country. Something more sophisticated for someone who would soon be fifteen. A Princess Di cut, two years before the shy English bride first appeared in front of the homicidal cameras.

Under my lovely golden locks hid a crown of darker hair, a post-pubescent inheritance, a saboteur of self-image. I went into the Dulwich Village salon a blonde and came out a boy.

⁓

Before landing in London, I thought I was:
  Female (but not girly)
  Tall (but not too tall)
  Blonde (like my father)
  Articulate (like my mother)
  Normal (though self-conscious)
I had never thought about the fact I was:
  Australian (not English)
  Accented (Australian, not English)
  Middle-class (not working class)
  White (not black like most of the kids at my school)
It turned out I was also:
  Androgynous
  Enormous
  Brunette
  Incomprehensible
  Different
In London I was an Austr-alien. My parents interpreted my dark moods as sulkiness and/or ingratitude. After all, not every fourteen-year-old had the opportunity to travel and live in Europe (Europe! Where history is more historical, where people ride around with baguettes in their bicycle baskets, where horizons can be widened).

Shyness left me lonely. I spent most lunchtimes in the library, reading Jane Austen. It wasn't that my fellow students were particularly unfriendly. I was irrelevant to them. After their initial curiosity faded, I became invisible. And I couldn't work up the courage to try and insert myself into the tight little cliques that formed the social ecosystem of this vast comprehensive school.

One day in a sociology class, towards the end of my five months at Kingsdale Comprehensive, a girl called Marie with an exotic French-sounding surname (her father was from Mauritius) invited me to come 'darn the chipper' with her and her mates after school. Even five months in, those words made no sense to me. Was it a sewing club? Something for birdwatchers? I hadn't a clue. I was so grateful for the invitation that I accepted.

And immediately panicked.

I couldn't sew. I didn't know anything about birds. What if? *What if what if what if what if?*

My patient brother, who was a couple of years ahead of me in the same school and apparently coping better with this strange new world, translated for me: 'She means the fish 'n' chip shop. Down the chipper. For some chips.'

So after school the next day I handed my briefcase full of clarinets to David to take home for me and followed Marie to the high street. I hovered awkwardly in the semi-dark outside the front of the chipper, nibbling on hot chips, saying almost nothing, while my new friend chatted with a group of white boys from our class. I watched as she sidled closer to the tallest lad, twirling her hair around her fingers, making him laugh with her vocab of filthy French words. Trapped in my alien man-woman costume, with my newly short dark hair and my chunky jeans, I was incapable of flirting with those boys. I wanted to, but the vocabulary simply wasn't available to me.

About a year after my return to Australia, Marie gave birth to the daughter of that lad and dropped out of school. She wrote to me every few months in mutant schoolgirl Franglais about life as a sixteen-year-old married lady. It didn't sound to me like she was having as much fun as she'd had darn the chipper.

I have made half a dozen visits to England since that first sojourn as a fourteen-year-old. Each time a pall of misery has descended on me, like the early twilight that fell as I walked home from school that winter. Even if I've been *having a lovely time, wish you were here*, visiting old friends, strolling the city streets with Tom, some part of my brain has always been sucked back to that London lockdown.

My thoughts turned to the Austr-alien girl at Kingsdale Comprehensive as I sat there at the social anxiety seminar in the hotel conference room full of mirrors. The psychologist told us that shy people have a neat self-sabotaging list of assumptions about themselves.

> If you suffer from shyness you worry a lot about the impression you'll make on others. Your mind circles obsessively around thoughts such as: *I'm different to everyone else; I'm weird; I'm going to be embarrassed when people notice me and how different and weird and therefore unlikable I am.* Irrational thoughts from a mind that imagines a critical audience scrutinising your behaviour. A mind that is constantly self-monitoring, creating a vicious circle of clumsy behaviour, social avoidance and an impoverished repertoire of social skills.

It sounded horribly familiar.

Mirror Mirror

The first time I removed a mirror from my bedroom wall I was nineteen years old. It was a plain circular mirror, the size of the windows on the *Titanic,* and it hung beside the door. I slipped my fingers behind the glass, found the thin metal chain and lifted it off the nail. I climbed on a chair and slid the mirror on top of the wardrobe, catching a last glimpse of my face framed against the ceiling as I pushed it out of view. From now on, whenever I left the privacy of my room, I would have to be myself, not who I was trying to present myself to be. That was the theory, anyway.

I was at university, a place where I had expected finally to feel like a grown-up, where I would magically shed this feeling of not quite belonging in the world. This had turned out to be a fantasy, and checking how I looked before entering the world had become a habit bordering on a compulsion.

I was as interested in my appearance as the next nineteen-year-old. It wasn't exactly narcissism, though. In Caravaggio's portrait, Narcissus stares into the glassy pool with a foolish smile on his face. This pretty boy is convinced of his own incomparable beauty. By contrast, I rarely smiled into my little ship's window. Reassurance was what I sought, a guarantee that I was neither invisible nor freakish, that my face, my body, my being, would hold together outside the safety of that room. I needed to be convinced that I was still in one piece because it seemed faintly possible that overnight my left eye might have slid down my face to my chin, like one of Picasso's portraits of a soon-to-be discarded lover. I was reading Kafka, immersed in his oddly familiar world of frightened outsiders. *What if*, like Gregor Samsa, I metamorphosed overnight into a disgusting insect, scuttling along the wall to hide behind the mirror?

I needed the mirror to compose my features, set my expression, straighten the mask. I had to see myself as others were about to see me—or as I wished them to see me. If I thought it was possible, for example, that the dark-skinned stranger with the fringed shoulder-bag whom I'd been staring at in the university cafe might be ahead of me in the coffee queue that day, it was even harder to drag myself away from my reflection and get to class.

Twenty-five years later, my quest to understand shyness was turning me into an amateur psychologist. Sitting up in bed surrounded by books and articles about social anxiety, I laughed out loud as I read about a researcher who had invented a mathematical formula for the impulse that had been tugging me towards my own mirror image back then. According to the formula I found buried in a psychology journal, my mirror problem could be reduced to a small collection of letters and numbers:

SHYNESS = M (1 - p).

The formula made no immediate sense to me. Maths—I had

always hated it. So neat and precise. Every *what if* seemed to have an answer in maths. (There was one exception. I loved the simple mathematics of wave sets: the mental calculations you made to catch one. The quiet sea rising up and pulsing shorewards, first a small one [not worth it] then a medium [careful] then a large [maybe not] then an even larger [forget about it] and finally the one to catch, the afterthought, the steady, pulsing wave that gently picked you up and carried you high above its foaming froth all the way to the shallows. Waves ignored you. You were the invisible unself-conscious rider. I loved that.)

Fortunately, though, there was a translation for the shyness equation. Apparently M equalled the degree to which I was motivated to make a desired impression on others, and p equalled how likely I thought it was that I could make that desired impression. My level of *SHYNESS* would increase when I was motivated to make a desired impression but doubted I would be able to do so. In other words, the more anxious I felt about whether my chunky spectacles would be a turn-off for Mr Hippy Shoulder-Bag in the university cafe, the more shy I felt and the more time I spent staring in the mirror at those studious plastic frames, wishing them away.

Of course we *all* worry about what others think of us. Anyone who doesn't care at all is probably a psychopath. The rub for shy people, according to the experts, is the extreme level of discomfort and anxiety we experience over the impression we think we're making.

In my mid-thirties I was writing opinion columns for the broadsheets. A natural fit: I've always had a lot of opinions and print is the perfect medium for the physically self-conscious. One of those columns, about a fictional character called Magazine Woman, described the sensation many women experience of being shadowed by an imaginary creature of such physical perfection that she shows us up wherever we go—at the beach, in the gym, in the mirrors of change rooms in clothing stores.

I observed that we knew, in one part of our cynical, media-savvy brains, all about what a con she was, with her hair-brushing, her airbrushing, her waxing and teasing and plucking, her tinting and tanning, her rigid work-out regime, her dental and her cosmetic bills. We understood she was a 'pawn of the industrial/entertainment complex' designed to stimulate our desire for retail therapy and distract us from the real problems facing this over-consuming society of ours. And yet still she haunted us.

This fantasy woman was partly a way of venting my feminist irritation with the media's saturation images of unattainable female beauty. I had read Simone de Beauvoir at university: 'Even if each woman dresses in conformity with her status, a game is still being played...she is...the character she represents, but is not...she strives to identify herself with this figure and thus to seem to herself to be stabilised, justified in her splendour.'

But in retrospect, Magazine Woman was also a sign that, in spite of my ongoing campaign to banish the shame-ridden self-consciousness that had plagued me as a teenager, those feelings had never entirely gone away. My desire for a 'stabilised' self-image, my anxious quest for perfection, was still chewing up a ridiculous amount of mental energy.

Was she my ideal self reflected, like Narcissus, always just out of reach? 'She's in the bathroom mirror,' I wrote, 'standing just behind you...your greatest friend, your worst foe, your Nemesis.'

There was a time, half a decade ago, when I thought I had become reconciled to my image in the mirror. When I thought Magazine Woman had been banished for good. My brother's wife was getting rid of some furniture and she suggested I take a look before it went to the hard rubbish. I salvaged a long narrow mirror from the pile and took it home to Tom in the back of my car. Then I got out the power drill my stepfather John had given me and screwed the mirror onto the door of the wardrobe beside our bed.

Now as we sat propped up on pillows, Tom reading his Bible, me reading my library books about social anxiety, there were four of us in the room: the bookish couple and their mirrored twins. But only four.

With Tom beside me there in the bed, Magazine Woman disappeared.

Invisible Me

I began asking around, trying to work out if my self-conscious adolescent anxiety had been unusual or if everyone felt the same way at that age. Most of the teenagers I knew seemed so much more confident than I had ever been, including Tom's two teenage daughters. One night when they were visiting us for dinner I asked the older one about the kids at her high school. She quickly summed up the social cliques in her year with a neat list of shorthand labels: 'You've got the Fashion Girls, the Cool Guys, the Nice Girls, the Arty Crowd, the Sports Jocks and the Invisibles.'

At the last label I caught my breath.

'You know,' she explained patiently, 'the ones you don't notice much. They don't belong to any group and never really say anything. So, like, they're invisible.'

I did know, and could recall how often I felt like one of them.

One summer in the early 1980s I went away to a bluestone boarding school just outside Melbourne on a national music camp. On the first morning of the camp I squeezed myself onto the end of a long bench at the communal breakfast table. The dining room had high ceilings and leadlight windows—a Hogwarts set, although this was decades before Harry first slipped on his invisibility cloak. The long table was crowded with young people I had never met.

As I began to eat, shyness struck like a sudden palsy. The spoon full of soggy cereal started to shake and I had to put it down. There were two certainties in my mind, and they were perfectly contradictory. First: everyone is looking at me. Second: no one can see me.

A thin boy sat down opposite me and introduced himself. *(So I'm not invisible then.)* His lips were bruised a deep pink from the pressure of his trumpet mouthpiece. I blushed and stammered but somehow we managed to have a conversation. He was in the first orchestra; I was down in the third. He enthused about his conductor, who apparently liked to sing a line from the orchestral score in a high falsetto voice and then make the player whose line it was sing it after him. *(I would rather die.)*

The trumpeter was not handsome but he had absurdly long eyelashes. As I watched him demolish a dozen Weet-Bix, my gratitude morphed effortlessly into a romantic crush. This brought its own fresh bout of paralysis. And so communication became almost impossible.

After rehearsals I kept a covert watch on him from the other side of the school swimming pool, silently making lists of conversation openers:

'Bartok—the Concerto for Orchestra—wow—what about those muted trumpets in the second movement!'

Or

'Stravinsky—*The Soldier's Tale*—how HARD are those

rhythms! Do you reckon your conductor could sing the trumpet part?'

Or

'Thanks for the chat at breakfast. Do you want to marry me?'

If I had been invisible I could have floated silently across the pool, past the dive-bombing trombonists and the dog-paddling flautists, slithered up onto the hot concrete and lain there eavesdropping as the trumpeter chatted to the oboist with the long curly hair and the perfectly filed fingernails. I could have listened, and learned how girls with perfectly filed fingernails honed their small talk.

My parents had first met at the same annual music camp about twenty-five years earlier. He was a trumpeter; she was an oboist. Like me, she chewed her fingernails. Maybe he did too. They were both Methodists back then and they were both shy. It's a miracle I was ever born.

But happily there was a lot of *horseplay* around that same swimming pool in the 1950s. There were *pranks* and *hi-jinks* and *come-hither* looks. Maybe she took a chance and swam to the other side one day for a chat, or maybe he did. But somehow they got talking. He had a motorbike called 'The Eggbeater' and she rode on the back of it with her arms around his broad trumpeter's ribcage. He took up jazz. She gave up religion. They got married.

Together they produced one bold child, my sister Yoni, and two shy children, my brother David and me, who all played musical instruments. The youngest one grew up and went to music camp and met a trumpeter. We didn't get married. In fact we never even *got fresh*. Decades later, though, I am still absurdly grateful for our breakfast conversation (mistaking gratitude for romantic love became a habit of mine). In my memory it was an oasis of communion in a desert of social anxiety.

But memories can be lies.

Not long after I had started my shyness research I wrote an essay about my battle with social anxiety at that music camp. The essay was broadcast on the radio and after it went to air a female listener sent me an email:

> Sian, I remember you from those music camps. I was back there in the brass section. As a shy person myself you seemed part of the 'cool' crowd and assured of your place in the social hierarchy. What an arresting thought all these years on that the sense I had of your being unapproachable might have been about your shyness, not just my own shyness or my failure in all things 'cool'.

Maybe she was mistaking me for someone else? I rifled around in my wooden box of precious things and dug out my diaries from those teenage years, looking for the entries about music camp.

I made an interesting discovery: the social desert turns out to have been teeming with life. There were trips to nearby surf beaches with flocks of flautists. Breathless moments on the basketball court with a double-bass player. Late night deep-and-meaningfuls in the dormitory with a lesbian harpist. And exhaustion, constant exhaustion, constantly diarised—perhaps the exhaustion of the socially overwhelmed? Or the exhaustion of passing for someone you're not?

There were even letters from the long-lashed trumpeter, just a handful, written during the months following the camp. He lived in a different state and the letters petered out after a while.

But why hadn't I remembered that part of the story? How had I forgotten all the frenetic social activity surrounding those orchestral rehearsals? Which part of my brain had been editing those scenes, giving Shy Sian the starring role and leaving Sociable Sian on the cutting-room floor? Perhaps if my shyness had faded away in the intervening years I might not have retained such vivid memories of that shaking spoon.

My fellow music camper concluded her correspondence:

> Like you, my path beyond shyness has also involved
> putting it into words. By talking about it in the context
> of relationships where I am accepted rather than judged,
> it has moved from the 'zone of shame' into the zone of
> normal human experience...Thank you again for such
> a candid piece of writing.

Candid? Now I was the one in the zone of shame: ashamed of the gulf between my self-pitying memories of loneliness and the recorded history in my diary of constant companionship. Facts revealed to be partly fiction.

Nice Girls

This is what really happened. I often felt like one of the Invisibles, but each time the black hole of social invisibility threatened to swallow me up, some extrovert would appear and rescue me, some social comet in whose wake I could trail, enjoying the fizz and spark. My closest friend was often the person who told the funniest stories to the largest number of people at any social gathering, and I was usually happy to lead the laughter. People like:

Sally the netball star with her glamorous American ways.

English Marie darn the chipper with her flirty French ways.

Mieke with her Dutch cheekbones and her anti-authoritarian ways.

Mieke adopted me on my return from London when I was struggling to find a place in the social ecosystem of my old/new school. The gap left by my absence had closed over and at lunchtimes I was drifting around with a group of Nice Girls whose conversation topics tended towards male tennis stars and the girls' budding interest in Christianity. (One of those Nice Girls made contact with me many years later and reminded me of the time I announced to them all that religion was 'for people who can't handle the knowledge of their own biological insignificance'. Not Nice.) My repertoire of small talk on either of those topics was practically non-existent and I was still lonely.

When Mieke joined our year I noticed she was soon moving effortlessly between our school's cliques of Arty, Sporty, Nice and Cool Girls. She even found ways to make her cloud-grey uniform look fashionable, leading the trends in sleeve-rolling and hemline length. Somehow I caught her eye and she decided to make me her confidante and co-conspirator. As always, I was the approachee rather than the approacher. For a long time I couldn't understand why she wanted to be my friend.

Mieke was often in trouble at school, mostly (it seemed to me) for the crime of fearlessness. She was unembarrassable. She called me 'Prior' and introduced me to eyeliner and rule-breaking. And she banished my loneliness.

One school day after classes had finished Mieke led me to a squat Victorian cottage just a few streets away from our girls' high school. There was a red light on the porch and curtains over the windows. Mieke knocked confidently on the front door. When a tired-looking woman appeared Mieke smiled at her and said, 'Hello, we're from the school around the corner and we wondered if you had any work for us, you know, doing massages?' We were sixteen years old.

The woman looked us up and down, clocking our school uniforms, our long stocking-clad legs, Mieke's pert Dutch cheekbones, and invited us in. As we walked down the shag-pile-carpeted hallway of the brothel we peeped inside the rooms. Red satin sheets on king-sized beds. Clothes racks with lacy things hanging in neat rows. Ashtrays and wine glasses. My heart was thumping behind my breasts.

In the room where the cash register lived the woman told us, 'The boss is out at the moment, but if you could come back in a few hours, I'm sure he'd like to meet you. You do realise you'd have to do more than just massages, don't you?'

Mieke was all innocence. 'What else would we have to do?' The tired woman looked increasingly dubious.

'The boss can explain later,' she said, ushering us back down the dark hallway and out into the sunshine before closing the door firmly behind us. We hung on until we had run around the corner then fell onto the grass verge, hyperventilating with laughter.

I couldn't remember ever having done something so naughty. Mieke was my Bad Influence and I loved her for it. This was a whole other kind of *what if* thing my new friend had going on, and it felt like freedom.

Approach Withdrawal

Tom had gone overseas again. He was a songwriter and his work often took him away from home for several months each year. I hated our separations, dreading them for weeks in advance, enduring them by burying myself in work and writing him long emails. Now, though, the shyness research had become an obsession and the ever-changing pile of library books beside me on the bed was a distraction from the empty space where Tom's body should have been.

At the moment I was reading a book called *Emotional Intelligence* by American psychologist Daniel Goleman. It discussed shyness in a chapter on temperament, which Goleman described as 'the background murmur of feelings that mark our basic disposition...the moods that typify our emotional life'.

He cited the research of Jerome Kagan, who had studied the physical symptoms of so-called 'timid' and 'bold' children and found in the timid ones a neural circuitry that is highly reactive to even mild stress. They sweat more and their hearts beat faster in response to new situations. They are paralysingly anxious in company and they 'treat any new person…as though (they) were a potential threat', which sounded familiar.

Goleman, like Kagan, was looking at temperament as a biological given. To some degree, he wrote, we each have a favoured emotional range fixed at birth. But the question is 'whether such a biologically determined emotional set can be changed by experience…Can even an innately shy child grow into a more confident adult?'

I first became acquainted with the term 'temperament' two and a half decades ago, when I spent a summer stapling. It was during a hiatus between finishing my undergraduate degree in politics and heading overseas, and I needed to save some cash. In a sweltering university office I sat collating pages of typed questions before shoving them into envelopes. The envelopes were being mailed out to 2500 mothers of newborn babies, and were the first of hundreds of thousands of questionnaires that would be sent out over the next three decades to the participants in a new Australian study of temperament. I was there as a result of benign nepotism. One of the psychologists behind the Australian Temperament Project was my mother Margot. She had made a decision in her mid-thirties to change career from orchestral musician to psychologist and was part of the team of researchers conducting the new study.

I now know they were trying to work out how to measure this slippery 'temperament' thing. How early could they identify children with easy or difficult, shy or sociable types of temperament? Was temperament fixed, or could it change as children grew into adulthood? When I was collating the questionnaires, I was blissfully ignorant of those research questions—but they were about to become starkly important to me as I prepared for six months of solo travel in Europe. Six months of staying in youth hostels full of complete strangers; six months without friends, family members or my usual routines; six months of making decisions, alone, about how to fill every minute of every day. For a shy person, this was a bit like holding your hand over a burning flame to see just how much suffering you could endure.

My mother spent many years of her professional life analysing those returned questionnaires. (She was also the person who first tried to encourage me to behave like a confident child rather than a shy one. If I would pluck up the courage to go round the corner to visit my friend Sally, for example, she would offer to give me a reward. It rarely worked.)

Maybe Margot would have a few useful things to tell me about shyness.

In the front room of her Carlton cottage Margot and I sat down together next to the walnut piano that used to belong to my father's father, Stan Prior. As a child I had spent hundreds of hours with her sitting beside me at the piano while I picked out the scales, major and minor, melodic and harmonic—Margot instructing and correcting, demonstrating and listening, her busy brain no doubt simultaneously:

– deciding what to cook us all for dinner that night,

  – thinking about the oboe students she had to teach the
  next day,

    – planning the psychology tutorial she had to run the day
    after that,

      – pondering the latest journal articles on autism
      she had been reading for her PhD-in-progress,

        – worrying about Yoni and her smoking habit,

          – fretting about my grandmother Mavis
          Prior and her creeping memory loss,

– choosing the colour of the floor-to-ceiling curtain that would soon be installed down the middle of the bedroom my brother David and I shared, to stop us fighting over territory,

> – making a list for the supermarket shopping she would do after delivering David to his trumpet lesson on the weekend and before delivering me to my clarinet lesson, and

>> – reminding herself that there would be extra mouths to feed when her stepchildren came to stay for the weekend,

while I sat there grizzling about the difficult fingering for G flat major, and asking again why I had to learn boring scales and arpeggios and waiting impatiently until I could surf the slow rolling waves of triplets in the Chopin waltz I was learning until they carried me gently to the shore of that final minor chord.

Back then, overlooking all my music lessons, there was a framed black and white photo sitting on top of the piano. It was a photo of the very same instrument, Stan's piano. Sitting on top of the piano in the photo there was another black and white framed photo, this one an image of my late father Glen. And in front of the framed photo on the piano in the photo stood a quartet of Glen's loved ones: my sister Yoni at the age of seven with my brother David (aged two), my grandmother Mavis Prior (old) and, in her arms, one-year-old Sian, already avoiding the camera's gaze. A bevy of blondes, the progenitors and the progeny, the genes that came before and the genes that followed. The photo within the photo, the invisible link, all of us joined by this walnut piano.

Turning away from the photo I switched on my tape recorder and tried not to think about the fact that I was interviewing my mum. Professional Sian would have to conduct the interview with Professor Margot.

PROFESSIONAL SIAN: So what did you discover with that temperament study—what IS shyness exactly?

PROFESSOR MARGOT: It's a personality trait or, if you like, a temperament trait. An inborn but not immutable biological disposition. As children we all fit somewhere on a spectrum called 'approach–withdrawal', ranging from the most engaged, extroverted kids who are happy to be with anybody to the most withdrawn kids who hang their heads, won't pay attention and seem fearful and anxious. To find out where the children in the temperament study sat in this spectrum, we asked parents questions like: how does your child react the first time a babysitter comes, or if you introduce some new experience or throw them into a new group of people? Do they approach and engage or back away and hide behind your legs?

SHY SIAN: *I remember being in a crowded town hall a few years back, at the end of a public forum that I had been hosting, and meeting an older cousin who hadn't seen me for many years. He was shaking his head: 'I can't believe that was you up there. I remember when you were about four and you would hide behind your mother's legs. I used to try and get you to talk but you were such a shy young thing.' And I remember him as a beanstick-thin giant with John Lennon spectacles and a blue sailing boat he had pulled up onto the sand on a windy bay beach, and I could recall the shrinking, scalding feeling all over my body and the flap of my mother's sundress around my head and the squinting sun watching me and even as my—now grey-haired—cousin and I were laughing about the fact that he was still wearing exactly the same glasses, I knew that that old please-go-away-please-don't-look-at-me fear was still only a shallow breath away. But why was I still afraid? And why did it matter so much to me?*

PROFESSIONAL SIAN: But why *are* shy kids always hiding behind their parents' legs?

PROFESSOR MARGOT: Shy kids have feelings of fear and inhibition that cause them to withdraw. This has to come from some biological factor, from the reactivity of the nervous system. Think of a child seeing a Father Christmas figure for the first time, say, or if something looms up in front of them. With some kids the looming thing doesn't have to get very close before they will react, negatively and intensely and quickly. Others will take it in and think 'this is frightening' and then cry.

PROFESSIONAL SIAN: You said it's 'not immutable'. Do some kids grow out of shyness?

PROFESSOR MARGOT: It all comes back to where you sit on the approach–withdrawal spectrum. The more extreme the shyness, the more likely it is to persist. If, by the time you're nine or ten, you've been shy all along and you're still shy, then it's a pretty enduring characteristic. It also usually means you're going to be vulnerable to anxiety as an adult. But lots of kids are initially shy and grow out of it. The way the parents handle it can make a difference, whether the parents are shy or anxious themselves. It's hard if the parents are biologically inclined to be shy and are modelling shy behaviour. But if the parents model brave behaviour, then that can help. If the kids try to reach out and become less shy, it can become less scary.

SHY SIAN: *You're shy too. You're brave but you're shy. I've seen you with the same wincing smile on your face that I've seen in photos of myself, seen you duck your head when you meet strangers, like I do, seen you sitting quietly and listening while the loud folk tell the crowd exactly what they think. I've seen you happily lost in a book while the rest of the world rushes by.*

PROFESSIONAL SIAN: What about introversion, is that the same thing as shyness?

PROFESSOR MARGOT: No. Not all withdrawn people are shy and not all anxious people avoid approaching others. Introversion and extroversion are on a slightly different spectrum from shyness. They're more expanded traits—the products of temperament plus experience, if you like. There are plenty of introverted people, including many scholars, writers and musicians, for example, who couldn't be described as shy because they don't find it distressing being in the company of others. Their preference is for being alone, in their own world, but they're not lonely. They don't find their withdrawal distressing in the way shy people do. They avoid small talk not because they're worried about it, but because they don't have much need for it.

SHY SIAN: *That could be a description of Tom. He's often quiet but rarely seems anxious. Not opinionated, like me. He opens up when he's writing but in person he is always careful with his words. Sometimes I have no idea what he's thinking. Perhaps Tom's introverted, rather than shy. Or perhaps he's just keeping his counsel.*

Enough about the research, Ma—let's talk about your youngest daughter.

What do you remember about me as a shy child?

PROFESSOR MARGOT: I remember that you only played with a small number of other kids and that it always had to be arranged. You weren't like Yoni, who would rush up and make friends with whoever, and you were more shy than David—he would go up to a group of kids and introduce himself in a diffident kind of way, but then he would settle. I do remember trying to bribe you to visit Sally because you wouldn't spontaneously go and play with her. But that's not unusual, some people like to have a small number of close trusted friends and others like to be one of the crowd. And I remember you would get stuck into kids who were being mean to David. You would stick up for somebody you loved if they were in trouble. So obviously shyness was a really big thing in your head but not such a big thing in mine. I thought you were doing fine. People liked you, you were good with old people and with little kids, so I didn't worry about it the way you did.

SHY SIAN: *She's right. Little kids usually trust me. Ageing parents of friends still ask after me. Why is that? Because my guard is down when I'm with the very old and the very young? Because there's less fear in me?*

PROFESSOR MARGOT: But I also remember being really proud of you when you grasped this shyness thing, because I knew it was at a high cost. In your professional life, nobody would ever dream you were shy.

SHY SIAN: *So why do I still feel like I haven't 'grasped it', this shyness thing? Why am I sitting here with this list of questions, interviewing my own mother, for god's sake?*

Prior Print

My grandfather Stan Prior, Glen's father, was a printer. *Prior Print* it said on his homemade business cards. As a child learning to read I found this alliteration intensely pleasing, the popping plosives in my mouth, those two big P's like hot air balloons straining to get away. Stan's fingers were always stained black from printers ink and he wore an apron. My grandmother Mavis's apron had ruffles but Stan's was a manly apron, inscribed with the hieroglyphics of innumerable inky finger-wipes.

In a shed in the backyard of their home lived a black-and-silver printing machine. I say 'lived' because it seemed alive to me: a squat, wheezing, Nazi-saluting robot that sucked in blank sheets of paper and cardboard and spat out personalised wedding invitations and programs for Gilbert and Sullivan operas. When I first saw the poster for Fritz Lang's 1927 silent film *Metropolis*, I had a moment of déjà vu. That sleek metallic head staring out from below the skyscrapers, Machine Man, was surely the humanoid face of Stan's printer.

Stan was always old. Born in 1890, he had married my grandmother when he was in his mid-forties. Had enlisting in the First World War got in the way of him finding a mate? Or was he too shy for courting? She was in her mid-thirties when they married. Why had it taken *her* so long? Too late to ask them now.

Stan was still running *Prior Print* when he was in his eighties. His favourite phrase was 't any rate, as in "T any rate, whatever they say about Sir John Monash, he was the only one who knew what he was doing at Gallipoli'. Or "T any rate, it's time I got cracking to the old folks home to play my cello. Helps give them a bit of a lift.' Somehow he never thought of himself as one of the 'old folks'.

In Stan's shed there were wooden boxes full of tiny metal letters that he lined up to create an infinite variety of lists and labels. Paper napkins printed for the wedding of *Hilary and Raymond*, for example. Stan printed too many (or was the wedding cancelled? Did the bride take fright at the altar? Where are they now, Hilary and Raymond?) and my mother was given a lifetime's supply of these monogrammed objects. In our household, serviettes thereafter became known as hilary-n-raymonds, as in 'Pass me a hilary-n-raymond, would you, I've got tomato sauce everywhere'.

Scattered over the wooden benchtop in Stan's shed was a collection of red magnets about the size of matchboxes. I think he used them for picking up the metal letters. I called them push-me-pull-yous. My favourite thing was to climb on Stan's bench, line the magnets up end to end and experiment with the forces of attraction and repulsion. Slide two attracting ends together and the magnets would rush headlong towards each other like desperate lovers. Push a repelling end towards another repelling end and it was like sideways levitation—unsecured objects moving of their own volition—pure magic.

Often when I meet someone new, I am overwhelmed by something like those same strange forces—simultaneously. So curious to know everything about the person, so desperate to read their mind, I could crush them with my enthusiasm. Yet so overcome by my own self-consciousness and anxiety, I want to back away from their outstretched hand and I can't hear them when they tell me their name. Exhausted by the rush of opposing emotions even before I've opened my mouth to say hello. Filled with self-doubt at the very moment I am most eager to please.

Approach.
   Withdrawal.
Approach.
   Withdrawal.
Push me.
   Pull you.
Push you.
   Pull me.

I want to be alone
   I crave company
I need solitude
   I hate being by myself.

I can't breathe, you're too close
   I can't breathe, I'm so lonely
Leave me alone
   Don't leave me.

Stan Prior didn't want to leave us. He lived for more than a century. Maybe shyness had made him cautious and caution could help you to live longer. Take fewer risks and keep out of trouble—although Stan did take a ride in a hot air balloon on his hundredth birthday so he wasn't completely risk-averse. He even made it into the *Guinness Book of Records* as the oldest brass-band member in the world. After surviving two world wars (was he a cautious soldier or a lucky one?) he was still playing his cornet in the local brass band at the age of one hundred, though, to be honest, by then he was more of a human mascot than a fully exhaling member of the cornet section. Stan didn't stop exhaling till he was one hundred and two.

At his funeral the crowd at the church was so large it spilled out into the street. My sister and I, arriving late from a snarled freeway, couldn't get in the door. We stood in the vestibule and listened as the local mayor sang Stan's praises and the local choir, of which he'd also been a long-serving member, sang his favourite hymns.

Afterwards, out the front of the church, my sister and I tried to make small talk with our Prior uncles and cousins, virtual strangers since our grandmother Mavis Prior had died a decade and half earlier. But the threads that bound us together had loosened and frayed and we soon ran out of things to say to each other.

Small talk was never my forte anyway. Words were precious currency, I told myself. They needed to be lined up carefully, as they were on Papa Prior's printing press.

In fact, my self-consciousness was often at its worst when I was called upon to make small talk with people I didn't know very well. It was as if I had missed out on learning the formulas and platitudes that most people take for granted. Or perhaps I was so busy feeling anxious in those moments when small talk was most useful, I had never had an opportunity to practise.

My stepfather John had done his best to give me those opportunities. John had been part of our family since my kindergarten days. I don't remember a time without his loving presence in our lives. I do remember occasions when he tried to help me overcome my fear of strangers. On summer holidays, cruising through bleached country towns in John's latest new car, the vinyl seats still smelling of the factory floor, there would be an inevitable search for public toilets. Slowing the car beside a perambulating local, John would instruct me to 'roll down the window, Sian, ask him where the loos are', and every time I would refuse. Speak with someone I don't know? In a place I've never been before? About TOILETS? I'd rather chew my own arm off.

Frustrated and busting, he would try my mother next—'Just ask him, Margot, quick, before he nicks into a shop,' and, like me, shy Margot would often protest, 'No, *you* ask him, John.' It would be left to my brother David, also reluctant but usually more accommodating, to make the approach.

John had more success in teaching me practical skills. How to use a power drill. How to start a recalcitrant mower. How to make mashed potato patties from leftovers. How to change a tyre. How to bluff mechanics into thinking I knew more about car engines than I did, so they wouldn't take advantage of the fact I was female. How to climb into the cab of a Mack truck in two easy steps. How to make a raspberry lemonade spider. How to cradle an injured possum in the palm of your hand. How to make Margot laugh.

John never stopped encouraging me to approach strangers but he rarely succeeded. It must have been baffling for him. What was wrong with this family? Other humans are not aliens and if they're locals they generally know exactly where the nearest public toilets are. For my stepfather, small talk was as effortless as breathing and almost as necessary. His job as a truck salesman required him to win the confidence of strangers every day and there is nothing more winning than an easy social manner. He could talk to anyone, any time, about practically anything, especially if it was anything practical. Cars, trucks, bicycles, boats, livestock, crops, weather, How Things Work, these were all fertile conversational territory for someone as socially skilled as John. His sisters, my country aunts, were even better. Words came spilling from their mouths like baroque cadenzas as soon as you answered the phone and heard the STD beep beep beep.

Don't get me wrong. Around the dinner table at home we could be as noisy as the next fractious blended family. But as soon as John drove us away from our domestic comfort zone, he found himself in the midst of a tribe of near-mutes. If raising someone else's child is a valid way of measuring the relative impacts of nature and nurture, in this instance nurture simply couldn't get a look-in. At the time, John's modelling of non-shy behaviour appeared to be having no impact on my idiotic fears.

Small Talk

At the age of fifteen I wrote a poem about my maternal grandfather Lloyd Jones. It rhymed with pedantic precision, vowels and syllables carefully matched at the end of every line. Lloyd's wife, my extrovert grandmother Peg, insisted on showing the poem to everyone in the extended family and to practically everyone they had ever met. I remember being a little worried about what Grandpa would think of me describing him as 'taciturn'. Still, it was a pretty impressive word and for a while there I thought perhaps I had the makings of a poetic genius.

When Peg died in 2009, one of my aunts discovered a copy of that poem among my grandmother's papers and I found that my pompous fifteen-year-old self had described Grandpa Lloyd as a man with a 'taciturn manner of speech'. My forty-five-year-old self enjoyed the unintentional oxymoron.

Peg and Lloyd lived in the same beachside suburb as our family when I was growing up and every now and then Lloyd would drop by during his daily constitutional and ask me to play something on the piano or the clarinet. He would sit quietly on the couch, eyes closed, hands clasped in front of him, fingertips tapping gently in time with the music, until the piece was finished. Then he would offer me a lopsided smile and a few brief words—'Lovely, dear, you play so musically, keep it up'—before striding off again, hands clasped behind his back, to continue his solitary walk along the beach path.

Tom often reminded me of Grandpa Lloyd. Neither of them had a lot to say at large social gatherings but when either of them spoke I listened carefully, and when their speech involved praise I stored it away in my memory.

As a young man Grandpa Lloyd played the organ in church and had a sweet baritone singing voice. Most of his brothers and cousins and nephews sang too—most of them terrible *show-offs*, according to Lloyd—ready to deliver a Gilbert and Sullivan duet at the drop of a hat. By the time I was fifteen and waxing poetic about him, Grandpa Lloyd never sang in public. I suspect his reasoning was that if it couldn't be perfect, it shouldn't be done. Or perhaps he was just too anxious.

Lloyd had been a high school teacher, eventually promoted to headmaster. Mr Jones had a reputation as a strict disciplinarian. One of his former students, a woman in her eighties at the time we were introduced, told me that Mr Jones once made her write out the sentence *procrastination is the thief of time* five hundred times. She could still imitate precisely his yard-duty walk, hands clasped behind his back, eyes alert for signs of adolescent time wasting.

In the Olden Days, Lloyd would have been described as *gruff*. He was often abrupt, especially with his wife. Although we loved him, I suspect we were all a little frightened of him. What I didn't understand at fifteen, but what seems obvious to me now, is that Lloyd was shy. And he didn't do small talk.

As a shy teenager I developed a list of justifications for why small talk was beneath me. It was tedious talk. Repetitious talk. Work-avoiding talk. Unoriginal talk. Talk for people with poor vocabularies. Talk for people who couldn't cut to the chase. I crossed the street many times to avoid having to engage in small talk. Once I even climbed a tall ladder at a party to avoid having to try.

It certainly wasn't that I hadn't felt the need for it. When I was stapling temperament study questionnaires for my mother in that hot university office, my inability to do small talk was one of the things I fretted about as I mentally planned my backpacking trip around Europe. It was a fear that would have to be overcome if I was to survive those youth hostels.

But how on earth did one do it?

What's happening?
What do you say to a question like that? I'm breathing in, breathing out, same as you.

What do you know?
Where do I start? I know how to count up to ten in ten different languages. Not as useful as you might imagine.

How was your weekend?
Which bit? Friday night? Saturday morning? Saturday afternoon? Saturday night? Sunday morning? Sunday afternoon? Sunday night? Could you be more specific?

How's tricks?
I wish I had a few up my sleeve. Like how to make myself invisible. Or how to do small talk.

Were all shy people bad at small talk, or was it just me (and Grandpa Lloyd)? Time to go back to the library.

The books on small talk were divided into two camps: self-help books and books by linguists and anthropologists who used terms like 'conventionalised and peripheral modes of discourse'. Both camps seemed to agree, though, that small talk had had a bad rap and was a valuable part of human communication.

American small talk 'trainer' Debra Fine was partial to the exclamation mark. She had even inserted one in her book's exhaustingly long title: *The Fine Art of Small Talk: How to start a conversation, keep it going, build networking skills and leave a positive impression!* Clearly Debra wasn't short of a word or two.

There was a dedication in the front of the book to her husband whom she described as 'the gentle wind beneath my wings'. At this point I nearly stopped reading. Originality in language use was not going to be Debra's strong suit. But then again, small talk wasn't meant to be about originality. Perhaps the fear of being platitudinous had been one of my biggest hurdles.

More interesting was Fine's self-description as someone who grew up quiet and shy, the 'reticent kind who sat invisible in the back of the class, often excluded', who withdrew into a world of books and 'had no idea how to make a friend or have a friend'. Consequently, Fine explained, she never learned how to talk to her peers. She could have been describing the androgynous Austr-alien in London, circa 1979. In spite of her exclamation marks and the wind beneath her wings, I began to warm to Debra. She was a woman on a mission and I was ready to be converted.

Debra's strategy involved two basic rules. Number one was, 'Take The Risk: it is up to us to take the risk of starting a conversation with a stranger...even if we are shy.' (But *what if,*

Debra, *what if* they don't want to talk to us, or we can't think of what to say?)

Rule number two looked more promising: 'Assume The Burden: it is our responsibility to come up with topics to discuss... to assume the burden of other people's comfort'. Now you're talking, Debra. Helpfulness. I can do that. I had spent over a decade working as a radio broadcaster, hour after hour of speaking with complete strangers where it was my responsibility to start the conversation, keep the conversation going, steer the conversation in the direction I wanted it to go, end the conversation when I wanted it to end. Make the interviewee feel good about the conversation, make them feel engaged and stimulated and comfortable. Surely that was 'assuming the burden'.

Why, when I was apparently so adept at that particular conversational art, could a chat with a colleague about what she'd done on the weekend sometimes make me squirm with discomfort? It wasn't just about the subject matter, either. It was more about who I felt I *was* when I was having those two different types of conversation. Two different people. One was a confident, skilled professional talking into a microphone, being helpful. The other was just me, undefended. Being evaluated?

I turned from the self-help books to the books by anthropologists. They were on a mission, too, but theirs was to rescue small talk from being dismissed as mere *gossip*. In place of that sibilant, girly label they had substituted the rather spiritual-sounding *phatic communion*. It sounded to me like something out of the Bible.

WELCOME, ALL YE SINNERS, TO THE BLESSED HOUSE OF PHATIC COMMUNION, WHERE EVEN THE LOWLIEST LEXICON CAN BE RESURRECTED IN THE EYES OF THE GOOD LORD WHO RULES OVER ALL OUR DISCOURSES.

The Polish anthropologist who came up with the term phatic communion, Bronisław Malinowski, had something in common with Debra Fine: why use two words when you can use a whole bunch to convey the same idea? For Malinowski small talk was 'a type of...free aimless social intercourse...in which ties of union are created by a mere exchange of words...purposeless expressions of preference or aversions, accounts of irrelevant happenings, comments on what is perfectly obvious...functional in defusing the threat of *taciturnity*.'

No wonder we were all a little afraid of Grandpa Lloyd. His 'taciturnity' was a threat. But to whom?

Another anthropologist, an Englishman called Robin Dunbar, had looked at small talk through the lens of evolutionary psychology. Dunbar thought human chatter was a form of social grooming, a bit like monkeys picking insects out of each other's fur, and just as useful. In *Grooming, Gossip and the Evolution of Language* he wrote: 'If being human is all about talking, it's the tittle-tattle of life that makes the world go round, not the pearls of wisdom that fall from the lips of the Aristotles and the Einsteins. We are social beings and our world—no less than that of the monkeys and apes—is cocooned in the interests and minutiae of everyday social life.'

Einstein rang a bell. Wasn't he shy too? Googling Einstein + shyness I found a website called *shakeyourshyness.com*. There the famous scientist was included in a list of eighty 'painfully shy' people who had become household names. The website had a whole page dedicated to 'Tips For Shaking Your Shyness', including 'Conversation Topics—never leave home without them'.

'Brush up on current events and the weather' was the advice proffered, 'and anything else that might be the small talk you need to get the conversation going!'

Small talk—again. If only they had invented the internet a century earlier. I imagined Albert Einstein perusing this chirpy little website then checking his pockets before setting off to collect his Nobel Prize for Physics in 1921:

> Handkerchief, yes. House key, yes. List of conversation topics for the after-party, ah yes. Should I start with the weather? *Rained today, could be sleet tomorrow.* Or current events? *Jolly interesting news about the plebiscite in Silesia, don't you think? And presumably you've heard they've given women the vote here in Sweden? By the way, did I mention that I'm painfully shy?*

Strangely enough, it's possible that Einstein would have felt entirely comfortable speaking from the distance of the Nobel Prize–winners' stage to a thousand awestruck fans. As I had discovered, shyness doesn't necessarily hinder public performance, especially when you don't have to interact one-on-one with your audience.

Anthropologist Robin Dunbar seemed to have a good understanding of the approach–withdrawal tango. 'Social animals hang in perpetual balance between two forces: the centripetal forces, driven by fear of predation, which have produced the feelings of sociableness that make us seek out company; and the centrifugal forces, generated by over-crowding, that send us scurrying for the sanity of a solitary life.' Centripetal and centrifugal forces: just like Stan Prior's printing magnets. What a perfect way to describe those hideous contradictory surges of emotional energy I experienced when meeting people for the first time.

Dunbar argued that our primate heritage had left us with a habit of living in social groups as a defence against predators. Social grooming, including gossip and small talk, were valuable in that they helped to keep the group together. On the downside, some monkeys and apes used their social skills to exploit each other, in order to ensure their dominance in the group. Harassment was a handy tool for lowering the rank of other apes in the group, for rejecting them and pushing them to the outer edges of the crowd hanging around the local fig tree.

If you're not one of the harassing, bossy, rejecting types but instead find yourself pushed to the edge of the group, there'll be fewer figs for you *and* a higher chance a tiger will pick you off. When you're trying to avoid tigers, Dunbar pointed out, 'the edge of the group is never a good place to be'. Was this why I had been fighting my shyness for so long?

I remembered Margot once describing my father Glen as someone who always hung around at the edge of a social group, never the centre. Was that by choice or by temperament? Had he felt safer being on the edge? Less chance of critical scrutiny? Less necessity to make small talk with others in the group? Or had that primal, primate response kept him quiet and vigilant on the periphery as he monitored the shifting alliances of the other group members? The anthropologist Malinowski reckoned that small talk could defuse the 'threat of taciturnity'. Was it possible that my father's quiet ways had seemed threatening to those around him? Had he found, like me, that his shyness was sometimes interpreted by others as haughtiness or a lack of interest in the doings of the group?

Reading the anthropologists' theories on small talk, I recalled a time in my early twenties when my anxiety about talking to other humans, sometimes even my close friends, had led me to consult a counsellor. Monday to Friday I was entirely engrossed in my job as an environment campaigner but weekends could be lonely.

After I had explained to her the self-consciousness that would overcome me when it was my turn to take the lead in casual conversations, the counsellor recommended that I attend some group sessions. Assertiveness Training, she called it. I must learn to be more assertive. Move in closer to the centre of the group around the fig tree, Robin Dunbar would probably say.

So one night after work I drove to a big red-brick house in the suburbs where the group met. There were about ten of us, all seated in a circle, all no doubt embarrassed to be there with our shameful little social problem. All struggling with phatic communion and hoping to be saved. I was one of the youngest in the circle. The group seemed to be dominated by middle-aged men who couldn't look you in the eye and who confessed to being unable to gain promotion in their workplace because, it turned out, the meek wouldn't be inheriting the earth after all.

The group leader asked us each to say something as we went around the circle, tell a story about ourselves, or introduce ourselves to the next person, and I recall feeling completely out of place. Whatever the task was, it seemed easy to me. Surely I couldn't be one of these people. While they were losing promotions, I was saving the world. I had no problem speaking in this company and felt impatient with the anxieties of those who did. Why was I here? That night I talked away confidently to the assembled crowd of strangers, trying to help everyone else feel a little more comfortable, and after the first session I never went back.

Perhaps I was in the wrong company. I could 'Assume The Burden' of leading the conversation, as Debra Fine suggested, because I didn't feel like I had to 'Take A Risk'. It wasn't assertive-ness that I lacked. In spite of my shyness, in the right conditions I could be positively bossy (just ask my brother David) or, at best, an enthusiastic leader. So perhaps 'doing' small talk had never been the problem. Perhaps it was that I could only ever do it when I didn't really care what my interlocutor thought of me. When I could hide behind some kind of professional persona. When I was there to help.

And when Tom was beside me.

Psych Talk

Small talk might have been scarce in our household when I was growing up but, courtesy of my mother Margot, we had our very own family psych talk.

Ten Typical Terms

1. *Auty*: colloquial noun to describe a person with *autism*. Example: My mother's PhD in psychology was all about trying to understand the *auties*.

2. *Aspy*: colloquial noun or adjective used to describe a person with, or exhibiting behaviours typical of, *Asperger's Syndrome*. Example: That guy who just bought John's car might have been a bit *aspy*, given how keen he was to tell us the mileage stats of every car he'd ever owned.

3. *Learned helplessness*: a term used to describe someone who refuses to learn how to do something they're not interested in, or are afraid of, or want someone else to do for them. Example: It was time I learned how to catch the train by

myself to basketball training, my mother said, because she didn't have time to take all of us to our music lessons AND drive me to basketball every weekend. Protesting that I didn't know how to catch the train was just a form of *learned helplessness*.

4. *Self-actualisation*: a term used to describe the process of fulfilling your unique potential as an individual.
   Example: Unless I could get on top of my shyness it seemed to me it would forever be getting in the way of my *self-actualisation*.

5. *Disinhibited*: a term used to describe someone who is definitely not shy.
   Example: It was best to try not to be embarrassed when my grandmother Peg boasted to strangers about us. She did it because she loved us, my mother explained, and because she was *disinhibited*.

6. *CBT (cognitive behaviour therapy)*: a term used to describe a therapeutic approach that aims to change dysfunctional thoughts, emotions and behaviours.
   Example: If I had been able to change my *what if*s into *so whats* when I was worrying about visiting Sally, it would have been an example of what CBT experts describe as replacing 'unhelpful thinking' with 'realistic thinking'.

7. *Labile*: a term used to describe someone perceived as unusually emotional.
   Example: After Peg got together with her new beau when she was in her eighties, she became much more *labile*.

8. *Neg re*: abbreviation of the term *negative reinforcement*, meaning to discourage someone from doing something by giving them negative feedback on their actions.

Example: It was best not to complain about the noise of my brother's trumpet playing, my mother said, because it was hard enough to get him to practise without the added *neg re*.

9. *Pos re*: abbreviation of the term *positive reinforcement*.
Example: When I was a child my mother offered to give me twenty cents as *pos re* if I would go up the road and round the corner to visit my friend Sally on the weekend.

10. *Positive re-framing*: (NB: not to be confused with positive reinforcement) a term used when someone describes something as positive or beneficial that could be seen as negative or harmful.
Example: Isn't it amazing, my mother said, how Peg always manages to *positively re-frame* every situation where she takes a risk, gets into trouble and has to seek help from a stranger?

Planet Earth

I found an educational video called *I Think They Think: Overcoming Social Phobia*. The filmmaker had interviewed three 'sufferers' and one 'expert' on social anxiety. You couldn't tell just from looking at them which ones were suffering and which one the others had sought help from. Through the camera lens they all looked perfectly normal.

> ERIC (in his sixties, a slim man with a moustache, sadness has settled on him like a shroud): I'm on planet earth, I look around, I'm with other human beings, and they're doing what I want to do. But I'm trapped here in this body and I can't do any of those things. For forty years of my life I felt that a cruel joke had been played on me. My body looks perfectly fine to everybody but in actual fact I was extremely disabled.
>
> JON (late twenties, handsome in a square-jawed, blue-eyed way, but his speech is hesitant): If you can imagine...being in a...constant state of fear. Rapid breathing, muscle tension, disassociation...Not really

being connected or in touch with your true feelings. It's very demanding in terms of energy.

LISA (English, mid-thirties, with a loud voice and a nervous laugh): It's very hard for people to understand what you're going through until they're in your situation. Shopping is so simple to those who don't have social phobia. It used to wear me out. I'd be exhausted. Just horrible.

SOCIAL ANXIETY EXPERT (pale red hair, a sympathetic voice): We view social phobia as being on a spectrum. On one end is normal social anxiety, the desire we all have to be liked and approved of by people. Then we have shyness, which is a degree up from that. People are more anxious in more situations, reticent in novel situations, hesitant to take the initiative in social situations. With an increased level of social anxiety you get to social phobia, so severe that it causes discomfort or causes people to avoid certain social situations. It's out of proportion.

CUT BACK TO YOUNG JON: By the time I was thirteen I was very, very phobic. I had an inability to function in the world at all. My first experience of a panic attack was on a Saturday evening. I went to a social event, got to the door and ran away.

Me too, Jon, I told the television screen. *I ran away from a party too.*

BACK TO LOUD LISA: I used to have to take my little boy shopping with me so he'd be the centre of attention. I couldn't make eye contact with the woman in the shop. Had to use my little boy to give her the money. I'd walk out with horrific headaches and a hot flush.

BACK TO ERIC: I had these problems all through my teens, twenties and early forties. I didn't have the skills so I was continually banging my head against a brick wall, making no progress…We all are extraordinary but social phobia took that away from me. I had no sense of the wonder of being a human being.

Next the social anxiety expert talked about something called 'graded exposure therapy', where you deliberately expose yourself to situations you fear, starting with the least frightening then moving through to the hardest of all. Eric described forcing himself to drive to the hall where the bush dance would be held, just to 'get to know the lay of the land'. On his next attempt, he might manage to go inside and have a dance. It was all about planning, making yourself a list of scary things you could work your way through.

At the end of the video the filmmaker wanted us to know that Eric was A Success Story. He could now go to a social gathering without having to leave immediately.

But you'll never get those years back, Eric, I told the hissing, snowy screen.

With a bit of research I tracked down the redheaded anxiety expert who had been interviewed on the video:

Professor Ronald M Rapee
Department of Psychology
Macquarie University
Expert in anxiety and cognitive behaviour therapy
Qualifications: PhD

What a lovely set of rhymes. They reminded me of an A. A. Milne poem called 'Disobedience' that Margot used to read to us when we were children. It's about an anxious three-year-old with the unlikely moniker of James James Morrison Morrison Weatherby George Dupree, who looked after his mother diligently until the day she went out without him and never came home again.

Which reminded me in turn of my father who walked down to the edge of the sea. My five-year-old sister asked our mother if he would be coming back as she watched him entering the surf. Or so the story goes. Sometimes, it seems, a child's anxiety can be prescient rather than neurotic.

Professor Ron was flying to Melbourne for a work meeting and agreed to meet with me in a city cafe. On the appointed morning I was running late and feeling flustered (shy) and for the first couple of minutes of our conversation I wasn't really listening. You are a journalist, I told myself. This is an interview. Get a grip.

Professor Ron had pale skin to go with his red hair. I wondered if he was a blusher. Maybe Professor Ron was shy too.

PROFESSIONAL SIAN: When did psychology researchers first start looking seriously at social anxiety?

PROFESSOR RON: The history of social anxiety as a recognised clinical condition is quite recent. In 1980 the DSM III (*Diagnostic and Statistical Manual of Mental Disorders*) included social phobia for the first time as a diagnosis. Social phobia and social anxiety had been talked about for decades, for centuries even, but to become of interest to research people in psychiatry, psychology, mental health, it has to officially get in the book. So all of a sudden everyone went, 'Ooh, interesting, there's a real disorder,' even though everyone knew that already. It had a lot to do with Isaac Marks, a British psychiatrist who did work on panic attacks, anxiety, panic disorder and agoraphobia. His group was the first lot who started using the words 'social phobia' as opposed to just 'shyness', differentiating it from the literature that talked about shyness as a broad personality style. He said, 'No, we can treat it, we can do something about this disorder.'

SHY SIAN: *Ah the mysterious power of taxonomy. Name something, put it in a list and suddenly everyone takes it seriously.*

PROFESSIONAL SIAN: How many people are suffering from social phobia?

PROFESSOR RON: The latest Australian figures show about five per cent of the population could be said to be suffering from social phobia. You have degrees of shyness then at some point the Official People say, 'This is social phobia.' But deciding where the cut-off is is completely arbitrary. The statistic commonly used for shyness is forty per cent of the population but studies around the world show if you change the wording or criteria slightly, then the figures for prevalence rates change massively. So in some ways the figures are fairly silly. If you diagnose someone as suffering from social phobia, that implies a reasonable level of life impairment. The difference between shyness and a disorder is where it starts to cause problems in the person's life.

SHY SIAN: *I like Professor Ron. A man who is willing to describe aspects of his chosen profession as 'fairly silly' and refer to his colleagues as 'the Official People'. I bet he'd understand all our family psych talk too.*

PROFESSIONAL SIAN: How do you diagnose someone with social anxiety?

PROFESSOR RON: The core diagnostic criterion of social anxiety and social phobia is 'fear of negative evaluation': worry and fear about being evaluated by others. A diagnosis requires that people avoid social situations because of that concern about being evaluated by others. A lot of shy people are worried about eating, drinking or writing in front of others. They have physical symptoms, like shaking. Those people say, 'When I pick up a coffee I will shake and people will say I'm weird,' or 'My writing will be funny, my hand will tense up and people will wonder what's wrong with me.' There are some people out there, very rare ones, who say, 'I'm perfectly outgoing in every other way, I talk to strangers on the street, but if I have to pick up a cup of coffee in front of someone, I'll die.'

SHY SIAN: *So my shaking and abandoned spoon at the music camp breakfast table might have been enough evidence for the Official People to diagnose me as a social phobic. Would that diagnosis have been helpful? Or more anxiety inducing? There was a lot of psychological jargon flying around in my family but I don't recall 'fear of negative evaluation'. If we had talked about a 'fear of neg ev', I wonder if I would have been able to stop dreading it so much.*

PROFESSIONAL SIAN: Has anyone looked at the question of whether shy people are particularly bad at small talk?

PROFESSOR RON: There's an ongoing argument in the world of shyness research on this subject. One argument says that for people with social phobia or anxiety the problem is entirely about perceptions. You think that you're incompetent at small talk, but actually you're not. The other camp says no, these people *are* incompetent, they haven't developed the skills to do small talk, and part of their concern about being negatively evaluated by others is realistic. My view is that it's all perception. Socially anxious people are perfectly competent at small talk but they perceive themselves as incompetent. If they don't perform very well at small talk it's probably a result of the anxiety rather than the cause of the anxiety.

PROFESSIONAL SIAN: Where do shyness, social anxiety and social phobia intersect?

70

PROFESSOR RON: It's a spectrum. Shyness is not exactly the same as social phobia. The clinical disorder and the temperament personality are different. You can get some highly shy people who get on with life and don't let it stop them. But people who are highly shy are the ones most likely to be socially phobic, and it can manifest in so many different ways. An interesting one came up in a phone conversation I had yesterday. The medical name is paruresis and it means an inability to urinate in front of people. I remember one case many years ago, a salesman who was extremely outgoing, he'd go up to anyone, sold fridges, no problems. But he couldn't use a toilet outside his own house. He had to make sure he had appointments near his home and he couldn't travel interstate. It was very debilitating, and bad for sales.

SHY SIAN: *I knew a bloke whose life was a bit like this, Professor Ron. Come to think of it, I know quite a bit about how phobias can shut a person down. I could give you an eyewitness account.*

Unsent Letter

Dear Andre (aka Mr Hippy Shoulder Bag),

I'm swimming out beyond the breakers at Coogee Beach and I see a sleek black head emerge from the water thirty metres away and it's you, it's definitely you. I'd recognise the shape of your head anywhere, even out here where the horizon lurches like a wire-walker's pole.

Except of course it can't be you. Not just because you can't swim (you never learned and you wouldn't let me teach you) but because you would never be here, so far from home. You wouldn't even make it to the airport.

But the colours and shapes of you must be imprinted on my mind like those hidden 3D Magic Eye images where, once you've picked them out of the pixelated blur, they're all you can see. Even now, more than two decades after we parted, you're still popping up everywhere I go.

Backstage at one of Tom's gigs, you're in the food marquee, helping yourself to something from the bain-marie. Except you haven't aged at all; how could that be? In a supermarket you're ahead of me in the checkout queue, but you've grown taller and put on weight.

Tiger balm. Sandalwood incense. Dusty books. Chicken curry. One whiff of cumin and I'm back in your darkened bedroom, listening to you reading the poetry of e e cummings in your gentle baritone and pronouncing the Vs as Ws.

We talked a lot about poverty because you came from a poor country. I loved watching those wonky Vs forming on your lips when you were trying to help me understand how poverty had contributed to the civil conflict there. You said you would have gone back if you could, and tried to help put an end to the fighting. I would have gone with you, too. But that would have involved you getting to the airport.

I've been reading about us in my diaries—the first time I've looked at them for twenty-five years—trying to remember the details of my campaign to have you. Because it *was* a campaign, a series of strategic manoeuvres designed to outpace my own anxieties. Shyness had been a kind of palsy that struck every time I saw someone beautiful and therefore desirable, and your face was the turning point. Enough of the blushing and hiding, the faked indifference, the self-flagellation after every missed opportunity. Enough loneliness. It was time to get on top of this thing.

According to my diary, I even gave my campaign a name. I called it my 'New Social Policy' or NSP (that was the year I took Soviet Politics). In retrospect, it was a kind of self-prescribed 'graded exposure therapy'. I forced myself to approach you on campus, to engage you in conversation about whatever political cause was obsessing me at the time. And what do you know, it turns out *you* had quite a thing for political causes too.

Nuclear disarmament, the Nicaraguan revolution, ending

third-world hunger, we were in furious agreement about the urgency of these things. And every time we discussed them I got to study that beautiful face of yours in more detail. The Jimi Hendrix skin, the James Brown jaw, the Jim Morrison eyes, the James Dean mouth: you had all my favourite Jimmies covered right there in the one face.

You even wrote like Henry James, in long letters you would compose for me late at night when you couldn't sleep, describing the authors and musicians and political thinkers you admired and the books and music and ideological tracts you thought I should be consuming, and admitting that you struggled with shyness, just like me, and explaining all the reasons you thought we would be friends for a long, long time.

Friends? No way. I had to have you.

Eventually I did, and for a while there was nothing but strange new pleasures.

And in a strange, new, pleasurable world, there is much we don't question, assuming there are rules we haven't yet learned.

For a long time I accepted your excuses about why you couldn't drive the rusting car sitting in the backyard of your share house; why you wouldn't come to any of the concerts I was singing in, or to my parents' place for a meal, or to parties or picnics or political rallies with me. The fact that you were from another country, another culture, almost another generation (there were fifteen years between us), all these facts made me reluctant to question your odd and disappointing refusals.

I was in love but I was often lonely.

Still I believed you when you told me that the little blue pills you pulled out of the bottom of your heavy shoulder bag every day and swallowed with mouthfuls of sweet milky tea were to cope with the pain of an old spinal injury.

After I made fun of your 'pill popping' you didn't speak to me for a week.

Then, when you finally returned my calls, you were ready to confess. In a quiet corner of the university cafe, you explained that the reason you couldn't visit my parents' house was agoraphobia. The pills were Valium, prescribed for your panic attacks when they first began a decade ago, but now you were addicted. And not only had they failed to prevent the attacks—you still tumbled down a dank well of panic every now and then, heart hammering so hard you thought you were going to die—in fact you believed they had made your symptoms worse. But if you didn't take the little blue pills every day you would suffer from withdrawal and become very, very ill indeed.

Phobias, panic attacks, drug addiction, withdrawal; I felt completely adrift. Isn't agoraphobia a fear of open spaces? How come you could walk across the vast university quadrangle, but you couldn't get into my little orange Corolla and come to the theatre with me?

No, you explained, it was more complicated than that. Confined spaces could be just as difficult as open ones, hence your inability to get into a lift. It was more about needing to be in familiar places, ideally close to medical help in case you had an anxiety attack. As a consequence of all this, you'd spent the last decade of your life largely confined to approximately three square kilometres of suburban Melbourne. And it was no coincidence that those three square kilometres contained three of the city's best hospitals.

Once I had digested all this information—and it took a while—I started planning my next campaign. There was a strong tendency towards helpfulness in my family. We all loved a good old-fashioned rescue, and your story was ripe for a happy ending. Hadn't I just had an outrageous success in the campaign to conquer my own anxiety? You had been my prize and, like a gambler who's just backed a winner, I knew I could do it all over again. Only this time *you* would be the beneficiary.

There's nothing like being in love to generate a truckload of hubris.

I found a clinic specialising in treating anxiety disorders. I suggested strategies for gradually reducing your drug intake. I enticed you into my car and drove further than I'd promised. I even managed to get you to the beach one day, where you waded in the water fully clothed, laughing like a child at the circus.

But it always felt like one step forward, one step back. You wouldn't come with me to the anxiety clinic because it was too far away. You couldn't go back to the beach because you had checked in the street directory and there were no hospitals nearby.

Meanwhile, I was learning many new and interesting things about the human mind. I learned that it was possible to develop a phobia about literally anything, from ablutophobia (fear of washing) and zelophobia (fear of jealousy) to scelerophobia (fear of bad men).

I learned about the fear of fear (phobophobia), and how it can bring a person to their knees as violently as a physical assault. I learned how hard it is to hang on to your dignity when the simplest requests from someone you love are impossible to grant. I learned about the intricate craft of lying that a phobic person must learn in order to hide their shameful anxieties from the world. And I learned that love can't survive on a constant diet of disappointments.

Do you remember that poem you wrote about falling in love with me, dashing it off on a scrap of paper one night and handing it over without saying a word? A taut tender poem about spring and the colour of my eyes. Mr e e cummings could learn a bit from this guy, I thought to myself.

And do you remember, a few years later, the day we were in a group of people watching a decade-old video of your best friend's wedding? How we listened to the speech in which your friend told the story of how you'd helped him woo his wife-to-be by penning a beautiful love poem for him to give to her? And how you became agitated and tried to get someone to stop the video? But no one would, and then on the screen the groom started reading out the poem and it was all about spring and the colour of her eyes. I was sitting there beside you feeling nauseated with the shock of it, the betrayal, the tawdry pre-loved moth-eaten trickery of it all, and we couldn't look at each other for hours afterwards.

Shyness isn't the only reason it can be hard to meet someone's eyes.

We lasted nearly five years, you and I, and we ended with a whimper, not a bang—a painful, protracted withdrawal. No matter how trapped I felt by your fear and its bewildering prohibitions, I never stopped wanting you. Sex was the one arena where your fears receded and you knew exactly what you were doing. Relinquishing that pleasure gave me some belated insight into how hard it was to kick a drug addiction.

But over the ensuing decade, when we occasionally met up for a cup of sweet tea, I couldn't stop myself offering yet more advice and solutions for your 'problem', as I still saw it. Compulsive helpfulness is a hard habit to kick, too.

It's been a while now since we've been in touch and I've learned a bit in that time: that we're all afraid of something, and we're all battling with or accommodating those fears as best we can. In spite of the success of my New Social Policy circa 1984, shyness still challenges me to a daily arm-wrestle. I don't always win. And a quarter-century on, the fact that my love couldn't cure you of a severe anxiety disorder still feels like a failure.

Who knows? Maybe that really *was* you swimming out beyond the Coogee breakers, enjoying the last hours of your Sydney holiday before catching a cab to the airport. Transfixed by the dip and sway of the horizon, and by the knowledge that the distance between you and it is no longer infinite.

I hope so.

Love Sian

Two Legs

Tom was away again. Another work trip, interstate this time. His absences were getting me down. I was in love but I was often alone.

Holidaying alone on the Sunshine Coast I dined one evening at a pavement cafe and entertained myself by people-watching. A frowning teenage boy wandered away from the table of adults who had brought him to the cafe. He stood in front of the blackboard menu, stroking the chalk letters until they were smeary, then swerved to the left and walked towards and past me. Stopping suddenly beside a light pole, he looked left and right nervously, as if awaiting instructions. Flicking his fingers like a pianist limbering up for a recital, he swerved and strode back to the blackboard to begin stroking again.

The adults ignored him and chatted on. I sipped my wine, enjoying the humid tropical air on my bare arms as I watched him flick and swerve, flick and swerve. And as my eyes followed him back and forth across the pavement I remembered watching another boy like this one, far away in a Victorian country high school in the dry heat of a southern summer. I was about eleven years old, which means it was the mid-seventies.

That boy had neat, wet, combed-down hair and high-belted corduroy trousers and he was standing beside the entrance to the school dining room, greeting people as they arrived for dinner.

No, he wasn't greeting us. He was oblivious to us all. His forefinger was on the light switch beside the door and he was pushing it up and down, up and down, up and down. He was staring at the ceiling as if he was watching an action movie at its climax. The whole room was flickering like a darkened cinema as the lights went on and off, on and off, on and off. I was feeling a bit dizzy. No one made a move to stop him, though. The quiet roar of conversation in the dining room was punctuated every now and then by a hoarse adolescent scream but no one looked up. I was sitting with my brother and some new friends we had made here at the holiday camp. One boy in our group smiled at me often. He had red hair but no freckles. He was one of the camp 'sibs'. I tried to avoid his gaze.

The formal name for this gathering was the Mansfield Autistic Centre Family Playschool. We called it Auty Camp. Our psychologist mother, researching for a PhD on autism, had been invited to join the families with autistic children who got together each summer for a kind of live-in communal therapy session. My stepfather John, my brother David and I went with her and while Mum was doing her research thing my brother and I hung out with the little gang of the 'normal' siblings of the auties. (Was I normal? At times, back then, I felt as disconnected from the people around me as the light-flicking boy. What made me so sure I wasn't one of them?) We roamed the school grounds playing chasey, riding bikes, occasionally retiring to someone's tent for card games and illicit gorging on mixed lollies. Our freedom felt unprecedented, exhilarating. A taste of things to come, here on the brink of puberty.

Mostly we ignored the auties (well, those related to them did; I tried not to stare but couldn't help myself sometimes, with so many weird and wonderful moves going on around me, the finger-flicking and head-banging and rocking and rolling, it was like I'd joined the circus) but every now and then we had to appeal to a higher authority when one of the auties took over the school trampoline and we couldn't get a turn.

'She's not even jumping on it!' we protested to the nearest grown-up. 'She's just lying there looking at her fingers, can't she do that somewhere else?'

Most of the adults were well used to this kind of arbitration (well over it, I'd imagine). They suggested alternative activities, like rehearsing our songs for the camp Musical Evening. My brother and I had seen the movie *Oliver* at the drive-in and everyone reckoned David was the spitting image of little orphan Oliver. He was going to sing 'Where is Love?' and I would do 'Who Will Buy?'

Love appeared to be on offer from the red-haired boy, who was called Jason. I was mortified and also flattered. Every time we played chasey, Jason chased after me. I was tall and fast so mostly I got away. Every now and then, though, he caught me (did I let him?) and he'd throw his arms around me and hang on for dear life. I didn't know what to do with him. Flirting simply wasn't in my repertoire. I stood there stiffly and waited for him to take his arms away, then half-wished he hadn't. We were both teased—'NOW I know your GIRLfriend'—and I resented him for drawing attention to me (*please don't look at me*). Jason didn't seem to care.

One day a big group of us—parents and sibs, mostly—went

for a bushwalk in the nearby mountains. The adults trudged up the narrow gravel road in clusters, flicking off flies with broken twigs and comparing notes on how to deal with their auty children's terror-tantrums. We kids soon separated from our parents. I walked with my brother and Chasin' Jason and a few other boys for a while, but then they all decided to jog. I was a sprinter, not a stayer, and I couldn't keep up with them. As I slowed down to catch my breath they disappeared around a bend in the road.

I walked on, swatting at flies, fretting about the Musical Evening.

What if the sight of people watching me sucked the air out of my lungs and I couldn't sing the song? *What if* I couldn't remember the words to the song because I was watching them watching me and worrying about what they were seeing? *What were* the words to the song? The fears flicked and swerved inside my belly. At some point I looked up and there was no one around. No one at all.

I waited for a while in the shade by the side of the road, thinking some of the parents might catch up with me. Had I missed a turn-off? Was there a map I should have been carrying? Had someone given me instructions about where to go when I wasn't listening? Why hadn't my brother waited for me? I walked on because it seemed as useful—or useless—as going back. At some point I began to whimper.

What if I was walking in completely the wrong direction? *What if* no one noticed until the end of the day and by then I was miles and miles away from Mum? My whimpering grew louder.

Eventually I came to a high bridge over a river and saw a group of people way down below, tiny people with tiny fishing lines. Standing on the edge of the bridge I cupped my hands to my face and shouted, 'Help. I'm lost. Can you help me?' Someone looked up and waved. They couldn't hear what I was saying.

I yelled louder. 'Help. Can you tell me which way to go?' Another one waved and shouted something back at me but I couldn't hear what he was saying. And I couldn't shout again because now I was crying and it was blocking up my throat.

There was probably a way to climb down from the bridge to the tiny people, but I felt too shy and embarrassed to go any closer to them. I stood in the middle of the bridge, weeping, knowing somewhere deep in my brain that I was acting a bit crazy. If Nana Peg was here, I told myself, she would just bowl up to the fishermen and persuade them to give her a lift back to camp. But the fear in me was too strong.

And where was my redheaded pursuer now?

Three decades later an email appeared in my inbox entitled: YOU WERE THE FIRST GIRL I KISSED. Getting creative out there in spam-world, I thought. Then I realised the sender's name was vaguely familiar. 'Now that I've got your attention,' the email read, 'that's not just a good headline but a fact.'

The redhead had grown up to become an advertising copywriter. He had Googled my name in an idle moment in the office. Jason reported that he was married and had a child, and enquired after my mother and brother.

Had he kissed me? It might be true but I couldn't recall the event. I couldn't even remember what had happened at the Camp Musical Evening. Perhaps the audience had bought my nervous first excursion into show tunes. Perhaps it had been a triumph and that was why I had been compulsively performing in front of audiences ever since. All I remembered was the bridge of terror, the miniature waving fishermen, and the unutterable relief of seeing a group of familiar adults emerge from a track beside the road about a hundred metres away.

Why do we remember our failures and sufferings so much better than our pleasures and triumphs?

Sitting alone at that Queensland beachside cafe, watching the boy with the constantly moving hands, I wondered about the world he saw between his flicking fingers. Were the rest of us like those tiny fishermen had been for me, waving at him and making noises, but so far away he couldn't make sense of it? Perhaps he was so consumed by the way his fingers looked and felt as they danced in front of him that there was no room in his mind for anything else. Or perhaps those hands were a comfort, something to focus on to combat the sensory overload of the world around him. Something that shut out the terror. Was my terror the same as his terror?

Back home in chilly Melbourne, I called Margot again. I wanted to know if there was any crossover between shyness and autism.

PROFESSOR MARGOT: No, there isn't. Even though they might have been mistaken for each other in the past, people with autism are on a different spectrum again to shyness. That's why it's called Autism Spectrum Disorder. Part of autism is being withdrawn and living in your own world, but that's not shyness. It's more of a cognitive thing, something about the way they process or fail to process the world. They may be very withdrawn because they haven't a clue about what's going on around them. In extreme cases they don't understand what these things are that walk with two legs, these humans, and why they do what they do.

So although I sometimes felt like an alien living among humans, I wasn't perched anywhere on that autism spectrum. I knew what was going on around me. In fact I spent way too much time with my social antennae fully extended, processing the world, worrying about what other people were thinking.

Shy Guy

At last Tom was back from his travels and he had brought me a gift. A new mix tape (on CD). The last few had been little spinning discs of musical propaganda, attempts to seduce me into loving the music he loved: first country music (it was hard but I was trying), then sixties soul (already a convert), Italian mafia music (hair-raising howls from the mountains of Sicily) and flamenco songs (hair-raising howls from the Moorish south of Spain). I was developing a taste for hair-raising howls.

This time Tom had followed me to shy-world. He had mixed together a dozen songs about socially awkward guys and gals longing for love and missing out on love and falling in love and losing love. From doo-wop to Brit-pop via Bollywood. I was entranced.

Ask—The Smiths

Morrissey made it sound so simple. And he was right. When you took away the complicated explanations about temperament spectrums and fears of negative evaluation and mathematical equations for measuring self-consciousness, shyness was just a stupid thing that could get in the way of you doing what you wanted to do. The Smiths' cheery little tune with its noodling high guitar riff and sweet harmonies somehow made escape seem possible, even inevitable. And I loved Morrissey's image of the buck-toothed Luxembourg girl smiling at her suitor's latest rhymes.

Tom and I had wooed each other with writing. We had met professionally a couple of times in the past but then came his out-of-the-blue email. Short and sweet, complimenting me on something I'd had published. I responded thanking him, and he wrote again. Those initial exchanges turned into six months of missives: sometimes one a week, sometimes daily. Sometimes he sent me his latest writing. Sometimes we exchanged lists, everything from Pet Hates and Worst Personal Faults to Favourite Books and Reasons To Live.

It turns out that email is the perfect medium for shy people. The pace of self-revelation is controllable. Distance spares you the agonising self-consciousness of social anxiety. There's just your busy brain and your tapping fingers (and your beating heart).

On the computer screen we could be nutty, nuanced, nonchalant. Nothing seemed to be at stake, nothing required except to entertain each other with words. We told each other stories from our past, we compared our reactions to novels we'd read, we even offered tidbits of regret about past relationships. Writing to Tom, I felt weightless.

And in one of those early emails, when I confessed to being shy, he simply replied: *As Morrissey says, shyness is nice.*

I felt like I'd been found.

Secret Heart—Ron Sexsmith

From The Smiths to Ron Sexsmith. Nice segue. Sexy.

Tom had introduced me to Ron Sexsmith's songs early on in our courtship, when my own secret heart was still full of fear. I knew that my hungry body was tugging me towards something my anxious mind still wasn't sure about, and this song seemed a perfect expression of the tussle between the two of them.

Sex was one of the things I sometimes felt shyness had stolen from me. Not just fucking, but everything that usually came before it: the subtle semaphore of attraction. My past seemed like a trail of missed opportunities.

The beautiful dark-eyed boy glimpsed in the stairwell of my first high school, his Adam's apple moving gracefully inside his long neck as he and his friends swore at each other in Greek. *Scasse malaka, gamisou.* Filth that sounded like poetry to me. I spent long lunchtimes waiting to catch a glimpse of him, then looking away if he so much as turned his head in my direction. Stricken.

The blue-eyed double-bass player who teased me in the break at youth orchestra rehearsals, making the laughter bubble up from my lower belly where I sometimes imagined him placing his big bass-bowing hand. There was one party where we sat on the sticky floor of someone's lounge room and that hand of his moved to stroke my calf and the blush went all the way down from my neck to below my belly and yet still, still, I couldn't move, my secret heart trapped inside this frozen-molten body. Locked in.

The dark-haired unionist who sang his lungs out in the trade union choir, *oh comrades come rally,* we were all comrades back then, I was Comrade Choir Mistress, but this comrade couldn't bring herself to let that comrade know that there was a reason she smiled at him in rehearsals and it wasn't just because of the sounds that came out of that full-lipped socialist mouth of his. At the pub after choir practice she watched him leaning on the beer-puddled bar, those lips moving, analysing the factional warfare in the Labor Party.

The workers united will never be defeated but this worker had no idea about how to unite with that worker. Desire was defeated by terror. And what was I so afraid of? Was desire defeated by pride? But why was admitting desire a matter of pride? Because the underside of desire is loneliness and loneliness is something to be ashamed of?

Arise ye workers from your slumbers, arise ye prisoners of want. Arise ye prisoner of shyness. Every song, every anthem a corny commentary on my infinite want.

There were exceptions. My campaign to have Mr Hippy Shoulder Bag had been a success. Just occasionally I could override the fear in social situations, reach out and give a signal that I was available. And sometimes, when I was far from home (or drunk, or both) and could pretend to be someone else, someone with less to lose, someone less hemmed in by *what if*s, I surprised myself with just how strong those signals could be.

On a train between East Berlin and Communist Krakow I once met a Polish environmentalist with liquid brown eyes and an unpronounceable name who asked if I would smuggle out his underground pamphlets. Then he took me to a two-room flat in the smog-ridden outer suburbs of his home town for the night, where he gave me half a bottle of vodka and relief from want.

At a surf beach on a faraway coast I met an artist who held my calf gently as he removed a fishhook from my bleeding toe and offered me two years of romantic respite from loneliness.

And eventually I was courted, from the back row of the trade union choir, by a dark-haired baritone who offered to carry my electric piano from the car to the rehearsal room and from whom I gratefully accepted almost a decade of loving kindness. But I was still hiding, sheltering behind a version of myself that felt somehow inauthentic. Still playing it safe. Still feeling that want.

And then along came Tom.

Sad Sad Girl and Boy—Curtis Mayfield

Curtis Mayfield's song about the lonely couple shyly acknowledging each other's sadness seemed to carry a special message from Tom to me—a suggestion that we were two of a kind.

What if you both:

- prefer lying on a bed reading a book to any other activity (except having sex)
- love that poem by Les Murray where he becomes the multiple selves of a herd of cattle, channelling the shit-streaming terror, the bovine 'us-ness' of them all
- spend a lot of time at social events worrying about whose name you're going to forget next
- know that if you're not reading a book or having sex, you would be happiest catching a body wave at a deserted surf beach (although every time Tom surfaces a little later than you might expect him to, you imagine the worst)
- love Curtis Mayfield and his sweet high keening voice that could persuade a nun to give up her habit
- like sending each other rhyming text messages
- laugh way too long when one of you concocts a stupid sentence full of rapidly changing vowels and tries to say it with a New Zealand accent

- say you hope you'll still be laughing at the same stupid joke when you're in the nursing home together
- like each other's family (Tom's felt like an extension of my own: same kind of people, just less anxious)
- love writing lists
- know it's not a good idea to tell anyone how ridiculously happy you are to have found each other, because sometimes the happiness of others makes people sad
- reckon you're shy

Hidden Place—Björk

Like me, the 'slightly shy' narrator of Björk's song knows all about hiding. About disguising yourself. And, maybe, about wanting to be discovered.

Not long after we got together I persuaded Tom to try the novels of Jane Austen. After he had read a few in a row he said he understood why I loved her. The silent observer. The outsider watching the humans interact. Sitting on the chaise longue in a long chaste frock, eyes narrowed, listening intently.

In return, Tom put me onto Haruki Murakami. I read *The Wind-Up Bird Chronicle*, and I remember there was a woman called Nutmeg and a boy who couldn't speak. There was a missing cat and there must have been a wind-up bird but what I remember most clearly was a man in a well. It seemed as if I had been down there with him, until Tom came along with a rope ladder.

Shy—Simon and Garfunkel

The poor shy guy in this song spends a lot of time in front of a mirror, wishing and hoping and sighing. Scared to death. I wanted to tell him: if you're shy the mirror doesn't help. In fact it just makes things worse. I figured that out a long ago.

Don't Be Shy—Cat Stevens

This song advises shy people not to 'wear' their fear. But what exactly *is* that fear we're wearing, Mr Steven Georgiou-hiding-behind-the-persona-of-Cat-Stevens-hiding-behind-the-persona-of-Yusuf-Islam? It seems to me fear is not singular but more like a set of Babushka dolls, always another one nestling inside the last.

Shyness is fear of other people.

Fear of other people is social anxiety.

Social anxiety is the fear of being negatively evaluated.

But what is the final, the deepest, the *most* shameful fear? What *happens* if other people negatively evaluate us?

Shyness is fear of rejection.

On the radio I heard an American pre-school teacher use the phrase 'the habit of rejection'. Her name was Vivian Gussin Paley and I found her book in the library: *You Can't Say You Can't Play*. So Vivian was a rhymer too. I liked her already.

I liked her even more after I read about her 'experiments' with kindergarten children. Vivian had noticed that some children in her class were habitually the rejecters and others were the rejected. 'By kindergarten,' she wrote, 'a structure begins to be revealed and will soon be carved in stone. Certain children will have the right to limit the social experiences of their classmates. Henceforth a ruling class will notify others of their acceptability, and the outsiders learn to anticipate the sting of rejection... Rejection in play is the forerunner of all rejections to come.'

Recalling her own kindergarten experiences as one of the

outsiders, Vivian decided to post a sign for her young students advising them of a strict new rule:

YOU CAN'T SAY YOU CAN'T PLAY

'I announce the new social order and, from the start, it is greeted with disbelief.' Vivian describes in hilarious detail how these little adults-in-training tried to find loopholes in the new rule so they could continue to exclude certain children from their games. In particular, they seemed to fear that if they couldn't exclude some children, they couldn't protect their 'best friend' relationships.

'Is the primary purpose of play to have and to hold a best friend?' Vivian asks. 'Or to establish who's the boss? If, indeed, possessiveness comes first, then how can any plan work that attempts to eradicate exclusive ownership?'

Vivian's stories reminded me of a grammar-nerd joke: 'I used to have a Greek friend called Apostrophe. She was so possessive!' I had always been the possessive type, always on the lookout for intense one-on-one friendships. Was that a shyness thing? Did best friends offer more security, less anxiety than friends of uncertain status?

I recalled hearing my nephew use the term 'rejected'. He and his primary school mates had been learning about the evils of bullying and how unkind it was to reject another child in the playground. Within the space of a few days, though, the word had morphed into a weird new insult, a freshly minted synonym for 'loser'. For example, he told me, 'When I drop the ball playing footy the other kids say, "Oh, you're so reJECted!"' What had begun as an appeal to the children's better natures had been converted into the very thing the teachers were trying to outlaw: the message 'You are not acceptable.'

I couldn't recall having been systematically bullied during

my own primary school days. Everyone copped it at some point, but many others copped it worse than me. I knew about rejection, though. The most painful memories were of my extroverted Best Friends losing interest and moving on to other Best Friends—more a downgrade of my emotional status than an outright dismissal. My attachments had always been limpet-like and I took these things hard. But it seemed to me that nothing in the history of my social life could explain the visceral fear of rejection that had accompanied me all through adulthood. Nature had simply obliterated nurture.

Shy Guy—Diana King

According to the narrator of this song, shy guys don't mess around with other women. They stick with you 'till the end'.

If you're shy, these things are important.

Too hard to start again.

Too much to lose.

What's That?

When I told people, 'I'm researching shyness,' they would sometimes hear me say:

    I'm researching Chinese

    Or

    I'm researching shiners

    Or

    I'm researching charmers

    Or

    I'm researching Sian-ness.

    Yes. I was researching Sian-ness.

Laboratory Setting

I sent an email to a Chinese psychologist at a university in Canada. He was an expert in something called 'shyness-inhibition'. I wanted to find out about shyness and cross-cultural differences. Was my shyness the same as the shyness of someone on the other side of the planet?

In the email I asked if I could do a phone interview with him. He didn't say no but he didn't say yes. Instead he sent me back a draft book chapter he had recently written. His chapter told me:

- the term shyness-inhibition refers to 'vigilant and anxious reactivity to stressful or challenging situations'

- in North America parents typically react to their children's shy-inhibited behaviour with disappointment and rejection

- Chinese children display more shy behaviours than Canadian children in a laboratory setting

- in self-oriented cultures (like North America), taking the social initiative is 'viewed as an index of social maturity, but display of shy-inhibited behaviour is considered socially incompetent'

- in group-oriented societies (like China) shy-inhibited behaviour may be encouraged because 'it may be conducive to group organisation'

After I had read the chapter I emailed the Chinese psychologist again, asking once more if I could do a phone interview with him about his research. He didn't respond.

I think perhaps he was too shy to talk to me. Or maybe too Chinese?

The Lump

In 1987 I graduated from university with an honours degree in politics and no idea what I wanted to do next. Things were messy with Andre. We were still deeply entangled and I wished he could come to Europe with me. I also knew I would have to leave him. I couldn't rescue him from his intractable fears and I couldn't live with them either. Stuffing the last temperament study questionnaire into its envelope, I packed my new backpack and flew to Europe. My plan was to cart that pack through Italy, Greece, Spain and Portugal while I figured out what to do with the rest of my life. And along the way I was determined to beat this shyness thing before it, too, became intractable.

After a few months my arms were stronger than they'd ever been, or have ever been since. Ropes of new muscles moved across my shoulder blades as I hoisted my backpack and trudged from the last youth hostel to the next train station. One of my toes had a permanent blister, a result of hammer toes, like my mother's: a cheap prize from the DNA lucky dip, along with shyness. With every step on the hot summer pavements I could feel a rhythmic sting move up my foot like a small electric shock.

The aches and the stings were only to be expected from a body being pushed further than it had ever been pushed before. Hundreds of kilometres of city pavements, station platforms, gallery corridors, cobbled town squares, circular stairwells, stony beaches, damp heaths had passed under my feet.

But the lump in my throat, that was a different thing.

A mystery.

A treachery.

At first I thought there was something stuck down there, a crumb of bread crust or a tiny olive pip, something lodged above my larynx. I swallowed and swallowed, swigging away at my water bottle, trying to dislodge it, but nothing worked. The lump sat there patiently, waiting for me to carry it to our next destination.

Some days it would seem to shrink—days when I found brief companionship in hostel dining rooms. Shiny-haired Californian girls with complimentary small talk: 'It's SO inner-esting to meet an Australian, I've heard you have a beaUtiful country!' Watchful Canadians with maple leaf flags sewn onto their backpacks 'so no one thinks we're American'. We would share stories about tourist sights to seek out and places to avoid: 'You'll be robbed in Naples, for sure.' The more I spoke, the less the lump bothered me.

For a few weeks I travelled through Italy with a Canadian woman called Linda. She spotted my grubby copy of Margaret Atwood at the hostel breakfast table in Florence and quizzed me about it: would I ever allow men to have the kind of power over me that they had over the women in *The Handmaid's Tale*? Linda reminded me of my sister Yoni—her peaches and cream complexion, her gesticulating hands, the way she cut straight to the chase. I trusted her immediately. And it turned out that, like me, Linda was running away from a sticky relationship with an older man.

We sat on the tiled porch of that hostel on the outskirts of Florence talking endlessly about these men, hers unavailable by way of a decade-long marriage, mine unavailable by way of a decade-long phobia. We found common ingredients, like secrecy, shame, unreliability, and always the feeling that we came second to someone or something else in our lovers' lives. And yet we both missed these men like we missed sleep.

Linda and I visited the museums and galleries of Florence and stood, still as statues, before Michelangelo's 'Lamentation over the Dead Christ', taking in that twisted marble torso, those sunken ribs, the strange gracefulness of the dead man's ankle. In my travel guide there was a quote attributed to the sculptor: 'In every block of marble I see a statue as though it stood before me, shaped and perfect in attitude and action. I have only to hew away the rough walls that imprison the lovely apparition to reveal it to the other eyes as mine see it.' Is that how we feel about ourselves? I wondered. We shy people? Like unfinished sculptures, waiting for someone to chisel us out from inside this marble casing of self-consciousness.

Linda and I shared a day-trip to Pisa, taking photos of each other in front of the tower with our arms stretched out, pretending to hold it up. We fretted about the black oil we had found stuck to the bottom of our sandals on the polluted beaches of Greece and about the begging children we had tried not to see in Naples. We shared our lists of All The Things Wrong With The World. As I offered her my theories about how it could All Be Put Right, I had never felt more articulate or more certain that I should try to Put It All Right. The words chased each other along my tongue and the tightness in my throat eased to an occasional flicker.

As usual my gratitude for friendship morphed into a crush and I desperately wished Linda would come with me to Barcelona. But companionship was always temporary in this backpacking community of colliding atoms. Linda had already been to Spain, and her money was running out. She had to go home to Canada. When we parted and my voice once again fell silent, the lump expanded.

Lying on my hostel bunk in the middle of the night I would feel it resting there, nuzzling at my vocal cords, teasing me with the possibility that it might spread out while I slept, and suffocate me.

One night in a train cabin where the seats slid down to lying position, loneliness threw a blanket over my conscience. A pair of newlyweds had befriended me, filling in the gaps in my fragmented Italian and telling me all about their wedding. Later, when the lights had dimmed and the rocking train had lured the bride to sleep, I felt the husband's hand gently stroking the back of my calves. I didn't move, either to stop him or encourage him, and as the stroking moved slowly along my thighs I could feel the lump in my throat melting under the wave of heat that spread over my chest and neck. So conversation was not the only cure for this mysterious ailment.

In the morning, though, when the groom caught my eye and winked at me in the narrow corridor outside our cabin, the lump was back again, worse than ever.

In Rome an overworked English-speaking doctor diagnosed the lump as a kind of spasm, an involuntary clenching of the throat muscles. He offered no theory about the cause but assured me it wasn't dangerous and prescribed some anti-spasmodic tablets. After a couple of weeks I stopped taking them. They made no difference to the lump and seemed to be wreaking havoc with my bowels. The lump and I simply grew accustomed to each other in the end, like my new shoulder muscles.

In a youth hostel on the Spanish coast just south of Barcelona, I was sitting on a narrow bed, feet resting on my backpack, listening to the murmurs of some young men in the next room. Their words were muffled by the door between us but from the cadence, they sounded like they might be English. I was rigid with indecision. It had been almost a week since I'd had a conversation in my native tongue and the lump in my throat felt the size of a walnut.

I had been travelling for six months and had had enough. I had proven my point. I wanted to go home.

The staccato sounds of the glottal stops coming from next door were unmistakable now, and I really wanted to know what they were saying. And yet they were strangers. The *what if*s were whispering to me again.

What if I couldn't think of anything to say to them?

What if they didn't want to talk to me?

What if they were quite happy with their own company, thanks very much, and didn't need some random Aussie bird barging into their boy's own adventure?

What if they could smell my loneliness?

I sat there in the empty room, armpits drenched, throat clenched, locked in battle with myself as one form of distress competed with another. Finally something tipped and I stood, took the three steps to the door and knocked. The voices went quiet and after a little while I knocked again and, without waiting for permission, I opened the door.

And the world did not come to an end.

Globus Hystericus

What had been inside that lump? Was it an ingot of unspoken words? Had my anxious thoughts tumbled down my eustachian tubes, slid down the back of my throat and got trapped there under my vocal cords, waiting patiently for a chance to leap out of my mouth and into the waiting world?

So much to worry about. So much to say.

TEN THINGS WRONG WITH THE WORLD, CIRCA 1987

1. Acid Rain in Europe
2. Apartheid in South Africa
3. Nuclear Tests in the Pacific
4. Uranium Mining in Australia
5. Rainforest Destruction in Brazil
6. Ozone Depletion in the Stratosphere
7. Indonesian Military Forces in East Timor
8. Nuclear Weapons in the USA and the USSR
9. Racism and Homophobia Almost Everywhere
10. The Patriarchy Absolutely Everywhere

After six months of travelling the hopelessly flawed world, this list seemed to be worrying me a bit more than my shyness. Perhaps fixing all these wrong things would be a good way to distract me from myself. I had decided what to do with my life; I would be a professional good influence. I was going to save the planet.

As a first step, soon after my return to Australia I applied for a job as a campaigner with a national environment organisation. I still remember that job interview almost word for word. It was as if someone else took over my brain. I went into the interview room knowing very little about the Australian Conservation Foundation's history or goals and came out charged with the responsibility of alerting the nation to the looming threats of radiation contamination, ozone depletion, chemical pollution and global warming.

Shy Sian had been abducted by aliens, leaving behind a replica, Professional Sian, to make her debut in the adult workforce.

Globus hystericus. It sounds like a perfect description of how the world looked to me back then. We were suffering from a kind of global madness, a heedless, headlong descent into political and ecological chaos. We had to be stopped, and I was just the gal for the job.

In fact *globus hystericus* was the term that could have explained my mysterious lump. Twenty-five years later a quick Google search revealed all.

'Stress or anxiety may cause some people to feel tightness in the throat, or feel as if something is stuck in the throat. This is called *globus hystericus*, or more commonly, *globus pharyngia*. Swallowing can be performed normally, but it can become quite irritating. In some cases the cause is unknown and symptoms may be attributed to a psychogenic cause *i.e.* an anxiety disorder.'

Of course.

Two weeks into my new job with the ACF I was required to speak to a crowd of twenty thousand people at an anti-nuclear rally in Melbourne's Myer Music Bowl. Again, I remember the details of that performance (because it *was* a performance: I was playing a part) with freakish accuracy. I was wearing a pair of blue striped shorts I had picked up on a Greek island a few months earlier. When the MC introduced me as 'a representative of Australia's largest environment organisation' I felt the invisible cloak of my new job settling around my strong backpacker's shoulders. My speech was ready. My cause was just. The citizens of Planet Earth must be saved from self-destruction.

As I walked onto the stage, leaned into the microphone and spoke the words that had been building up in me for years, the tightness in my throat eased and the last traces of the lump faded away.

On Lists

Three reasons why shy people might like writing lists:

1. Lists generate a sense of control over the things you're listing.
   Acute social anxiety, by contrast, can make you feel like
   you've lost control of:
   – your body
   – your emotions
   – your intentions
   – your mind

2. Lists can distract you from the whispering *what if*s by giving
   you a series of achievable goals, such as:
   a) say hello to the neighbour next time you're weeding your
      front garden
   b) accept the handsome baritone's next offer of a lift home
      from choir practice
   c) ask your work colleagues what they did on the weekend
   d) don't leave the birthday party early

3. Lists can be used to log your small victories in the battle against social anxiety, such as:
   a) smiled at Mr Hippy Shoulder Bag in the university cafe
   b) chatted to the woman working at the supermarket checkout
   c) accepted an invitation to the work Christmas party
   d) resisted the urge to cancel the session with the professional photographer

A strange fact: In 2009 the Italian writer Umberto Eco curated an exhibition for the Louvre Gallery called *Mille e tre* ('One thousand and three'). It was an exhibition about lists.

Four reasons Signor Eco is partial to lists:
   1. 'The list is the origin of culture'
   2. 'A list allows us to question the essential definitions'
   3. 'Lists make infinity comprehensible'
   4. 'We like lists because we don't want to die'

One reason why a shy person might feel embarrassed about writing so many lists:
   It might make them wonder if perhaps they suffer from obsessive compulsive disorder as well as social anxiety.

Some consolations for a shy list-writing person:
   Lots of people write lists, not just the shy ones
   Umberto Eco writes lists
   Tom writes lists
   It's probably one of the Hundred Habits of Highly Successful Humans

Goodness Me

So there I was: a self-actualising super-heroine in blue striped shorts. Could there have been a link between my hubristic plans to save the world and a shy temperament? I went back to the transcript of my interview with Professor Ron.

PROFESSOR RON: In our social anxiety treatment programs for children we talk to parents about how, on the negative side, their kids are prone to being anxious, depressed and stressed, but on the positive side, they're usually also very reliable, conscientious and so on. Shyness is correlated with high empathy. I'm sure you'd find that, professionally, shy people are often in caring roles.

It makes a lot of sense because it would take the attention away from you. In jobs where the focus is entirely on some other thing, it's off you, and that could make a shy person do something that's seemingly outgoing.

He was right. It did make a lot of sense. The imminent demise of the ozone layer had certainly taken my mind off my anxious self-consciousness, at least when I was working. And it should have been flattering, the way Professor Ron described the upside of being shy.

> HERE LIES SIAN PRIOR
> SHE WAS RELIABLE
> ALSO CONSCIENTIOUS
> AND SO ON
> REST IN PEACE

Blecch.

A List of Whens and Whats

When Mieke and I became friends in high school she stopped mucking around so much in class. She finished her homework more often. She tormented her teachers less. 'You're a good influence on her,' they murmured to me in the corridors.

What the teachers didn't know is that our torments (because now I joined in) merely became subtler. She (we) replaced her ear-popping, class-stopping pantomime sneezes with a constant high-pitched hum. School choir practice had given us both an extra few top notes; we sat at the back of the class, faces studious, mouths closed, and sent those mosquito whines straight up our noses and out towards the blackboard. We made sure our noise was just quiet enough for its source to be impossible to locate, but just loud enough to cause vague, constant irritation to whichever teacher was in charge. In this way Mieke could be bad and get away with it. And I could be bad *and* be a Good Influence.

When Andre and I became lovers he tried to reduce his daily dosage of Valium. He tried to push the limits of his agoraphobic comfort zone. He re-enrolled in his university degree and talked about trying to get work. His family was pleased. 'You're a good influence on him,' they whispered to me in his kitchen.

What they didn't witness was my refusal to turn the car around when he clutched at his constricted chest and begged me to take him home; the times he overslept and missed his lectures and instead got a lecture from me; my refusal to spend the night with him because most nights he couldn't sleep until dawn. Tough love. *Negative reinforcement* in uncompromising doses.

When Tom and I first got together he was an irregular heroin user. He was bad company when he was stoned. If I told him interesting stuff he just said, 'Yeah, whatever'. And I was worried it was going to kill him. I asked him to choose between heroin and me. Eventually he chose me. His friends were relieved and grateful. 'He looks so much healthier since you've been together,' they said. 'You're so good for him.' Even Tom told me, 'I like who I am when I'm with you.'

What they couldn't know was that when he slipped away one morning and allowed himself a little taste, I refused to go with him that afternoon to the wedding of one of his closest friends. 'I don't care what you tell your friend,' I said. 'Tell him I'm sick. Sick of who you are when you use heroin.' Hardline *neg re*. Self-righteous helpfulness.

When I first started researching shyness I thought perhaps I could write a book about it. Then at work one day I found a piece of paper left on the photocopier by another writing teacher. It had a list of instructions about how to write something called a 'self-referential joke'.

Exercise One: Devise punchlines that undermine or confirm their premise.

Example: Confirm—*I'm very shy. Oh dear, I've said too much.*

Undermine—*I'm very shy. Let me tell you about it.*

What it made me wonder was, if I wrote a whole book about my shyness, would anyone actually believe that I was shy? Or would they think it was a joke?

When I decided I would try to write about book about shyness anyway, I thought perhaps I would write a self-help book for shy people. I could tell My Story, offer My Insights, share the Inside Information I had gained by reading all those library books and talking to all those experts. By the time my shy readers had finished my book they would understand exactly why they sometimes felt like an alien amongst humans, and they would have some Useful Strategies for dealing with their Irrational Fears.

What I realised, though, is that I'm not interested in self-help books. I imagine they are full of trite phrases like 'being your Best Self' and 'undertaking the Learning Journey', phrases that reproach their readers for a failure to self-actualise. I don't want to be a Good Influence anymore. I don't want to help others. I'm not interested in writing a self-help book because, ironically, it's actually *self*-help I'm interested in.

When I say I'm trying to help myself, though, am I still trying to be A Good Influence—this time on Shy Sian? Am I trying to understand shyness in order to eradicate it because my shy self is not and has never been and will never be my 'best self'? Because I'm on a Sisyphean mission of self-actualisation?

What can you do? According to something Professor Ron told me in our interview, if you're shy, being a Good Influence seems to be hard-wired:

PROFESSOR RON: When we talk to parents who are worried about their shy kids we tell them that there are positives that often go with it, like greater sensitivity and greater levels of honesty. Things that are seen as 'good person' emotions, less self-serving emotions. With empathy, there's that idea of putting yourself in other people's situations. Shy people are often good listeners. So there are non-self-aggrandising, non-domineering positives that often go with shyness.

SHY SIAN: *It's true, I have spent a lot of time worrying about whether I've said something to hurt someone, been unsympathetic, failed in compassion. So it's a shyness thing, all that fretting about what others are thinking and feeling. How exhausting. And yet, when you say nice things like that about us—about me—I'm not sure I believe you, Professor Ron. Maybe my hard line good-influencing has been a form of self-aggrandisement. Maybe I wanted to make myself feel important by helping others.*

PROFESSOR RON: Shy people often discount positive evaluation entirely. They are more strongly attracted to negative evaluation information. When socially anxious people get positive comments from another person it often increases their anxiety at the next interaction. One study showed that where there are two people interacting and one gives the socially anxious person compliments like 'you look fabulous' or 'you're doing a great job', and later you ask the socially anxious person, 'How do you feel about mixing with that person again?' they will say, 'I'm more anxious now because the bar's been raised—that person thinks I'm competent but I'm not, so I'm really in trouble!'

SHY SIAN: *But empathy hasn't always made me helpful, Professor Ron. I have not always been kind to other shy people. In fact I have often been irritated and impatient when it seemed they weren't making an effort to fight the good fight against their own temperament trait. I didn't want to be one of them. They were the risk-avoiders, the failing self-actualisers. I wanted to be one of the loud ones, the assertive ones, the popular ones. And sometimes my social anxiety has got in the way of kindness.*

Not Helpful

You've been asleep for ten hours but you wake up and it's actually only been ninety minutes and what woke you up was the sound of the woman in the next hospital bed whimpering with pain.

Her whimpers turn to sobs that turn to groans as her head threatens to explode from pain. Where the hell does it come from? The doctors can't say. It looked like an aneurism but all the tests in the world, the MRI tube of pain, the dye of pain, the lumbar puncture of pain, can't confirm or deny their vague diagnosis.

So she's crying out for the nurse, who gives her Panadeine Forte, but that takes a good twenty minutes to work, and in the meantime her arms and legs start tingling and pretty soon she can't feel her hands, and who is there to comfort her? The nurse has gone away to page a doctor, and the woman is calling out, 'Come back. Don't leave me. I'm scared. Somebody?'

You're lying two feet away from her in your roofless tent, earplugs out, wide awake, wondering if you should ease yourself painfully out of bed and go to the side of this woman and hold her hand (*what if* she doesn't want you to?) and tell her someone cares (*what if* she doesn't believe you?).

You don't move.

You lie there silently and half of you is resenting your broken sleep and wishing she'd shut up and the other half knows exactly how she feels, how unspeakably awful this pain is, how you think you're going to die and you half wish you would. But you don't move. You just lie there behind your sky-blue hospital curtain, blushing with shame.

Eventually the pills kick in and she sleeps. But you don't, not for a long time.

In the morning you offer your sympathy, too little too late, and she apologises for waking you in the night. Somehow the night's dramas have opened everybody up and pretty soon the other two women are telling their stories too.

There's Polly who has five kids from three different fathers, but her new boyfriend is different, she says. She'd been having a holiday, the first day of a week-long holiday from her job cleaning in a nursing home where she really loves the old folk. She says they have a great sense of humour. One old woman, Gladys, said about a new resident, 'Who's that bastard?' and when Polly said, 'I beg your pardon,' Gladys said, 'Whose is that basket?' and smiled a sly smile.

So Polly's on holiday and she's kissing her new boyfriend and suddenly it feels like a small plane has done a suicide plummet into her temples and she can't stand up for the pain. Her boyfriend calls the hospital and she has to be airlifted from her country town to Melbourne because they don't have the technology to sort her out up there. The trouble is, they don't seem to have it here either. She's been through all the technologies of pain too, and they can't figure her out. She's also had a drip inserted into the wrong part of her body all night so instead of reaching her veins it's gone into her soft muscle tissue and her arms have swollen up. When the offending doctor comes around in the morning to sort it out, she apologises to him for causing trouble.

And then there's Beryl, whose son-in-law has promised to buy her a Frankenstein mask because that's what the new scar on her temple reminds him of, and she thinks it's a hoot. She's quite disinhibited and often talks to herself, and you've learned not to feel like you have to respond. Beryl got sacked from her job last week, by letter, because her boss couldn't wait the three months it will take her to recover (if she's lucky). So she's asking the nurse if there are any jobs for her at the hospital, and offering to go to a job interview in her nightie.

She asks you if you're married, or have any children, and when the answer is no, she and the others lose interest in you. You're half disappointed and half glad, because even though you could tell them some stories, none of yours could compete with theirs.

Even when you close your eyes you can't block out their pain and their after-midnight groans and their sad, worried children and their uncertain futures. You ache with the relief of knowing that soon you'll be out of here, now that they've chopped the protruding bit off your dodgy spine, but next week these women will still be here, propped up on their pillows, hair awry, mouths dry, waiting for the next round of pills and the next visit from the be-suited young doctors who hold all the answers—except maybe they don't.

You wonder for a long time afterwards why you hadn't gone to the crying woman. And *what if* you had?

So Lucky

Tom and I had a dinner date. After all our time apart in the last six months I was hungry for his company. Pushing open the door of a dimly lit Italian restaurant not far from our home I walked towards the bar where a waiter was directing people to their seats. Tom was following close behind me, and it happened.

The moment.

The turning of the heads. The torsos leaning towards each other. The gesturing with a sideways jerk of the head. The widening of the eyes as recognition dawned. The waiter was answering my question but looking at Tom, his voice oleaginous with pleasure. 'Not a problem, absolutely, one hundred per cent,' he beamed.

As we took our seats in the crowded restaurant, it seemed as if all eyes were turned towards us. And I disappeared.

Tom was famous, you see. Over the decades his songwriting had built an elegant but sturdy bridge between the worlds of high art and popular culture and his work had found a huge audience, even making it onto the high school syllabus. People often stopped him on the street to ask for his autograph and, if they were brave, a photo. 'Love your work,' they'd say. 'Mate, you're a legend.'

Mostly they waited for me to step aside so they could get an uncluttered shot of Tom's famous head. Sometimes they asked me to take the photo while they leaned in close, an arm around his shoulders, smiling proudly at the camera for their disbelieving friends.

Once in a bar in Norway where a small crowd had come to hear Tom's songs, a young man got the photograph with his hero that he had flown all the way from the Arctic Circle to get. As Tom shook his hand and walked away, the young man turned to me and said, 'Are you his girlfriend? You're so *lucky*!'

'Why, would *you* like to be his girlfriend?' I snapped. 'Maybe *he's* the lucky one.' And felt ashamed of myself as the young man's ruddy Arctic face filled with confusion.

In the beginning, I obliged the photograph-hunters. I smiled and waited patiently for them to get themselves into position. I clicked and clicked again just to be sure. Lately, though, I had become less obliging. Sometimes I continued down the street, letting Tom catch up when the fans had gone. Had the interruptions become more frequent? Had Tom become more willing to oblige the fans, less willing to create boundaries between his professional and private personas, to give us some breathing space?

Was it my ego? Did I resent not being the one who was having their photo taken? I famously *hated* having my photo taken; I was the woman who longed for invisibility. But not like this. Not now that everybody/nobody was looking at invisible me. Each time it was as if I was still sitting squirming at that breakfast table at music camp, wanting to be noticed, befriended, admired, but instead feeling insignificant and trapped and alone.

Oh for god's sake—I didn't want to be invisible. You don't agree to lobby politicians and do television screen tests and sing in recitals and host public forums and teach classrooms full of students if you want to be invisible. I craved public acknowledgment as much as Tom did. I enjoyed the adrenaline rush that came from pleasing the crowd in the same way he did. It was the self-consciousness I couldn't stand, the way my own mind habitually stood outside itself, watching me, evaluating me. The constant performance anxiety in the presence of other humans.

Alone, I could walk down the street and be just another person walking down the street, being ignored by all the other people walking down the street. In the company of Tom the scrutiny I imagined in my most anxious moments became painfully manifest as the eyes swivelled towards us and the whispers followed us down the street.

They looked.

I felt them looking.

I worried about what they were thinking.

I couldn't act normal because I knew they were watching.

I straightened my back and lifted my head higher.

I chose my facial expressions with care.

But I knew they were not really looking at me.

They were looking at him.

And I hated that.

I hated that their focus on him prevented them from seeing me.

Even though I hated them looking at me.

What *was* that?

Was that the difference between being shy and being an introvert?

Or between being a shy extrovert and an introvert?

If I had been an introvert I wouldn't want them to look at me.

I might be relieved to walk away and let them take his photo.

I didn't want them to take my photo.

But I wanted to be the one they were interested in.

Or the equally interesting one.

That's why I had fought it so long and so hard.

Found ways to have my say.

Pushed myself into the world.

I didn't want to be interesting only because I was with him.

But I wanted to be with him.

He made me feel interesting.

Interesting, isn't it?

The oily waiter found us a table down the back of the restaurant, away from all those eyes. Tom was quiet, distracted. 'Is anything wrong?' I asked.

He fiddled with a napkin, folding and unfolding it. 'The songwriting,' he said finally. 'I haven't written anything new for months. I've just been out there selling the old stuff. Slicing the same old salami. I feel kind of useless.'

'You've got some time at home now,' I said. 'You can write.'

'I don't really have any ideas. And I don't have that much time,' he said. 'I've been asked to another festival. Next month.'

There was a flicker in my throat. Everyone wanted Tom.

I knew he would go. In spite of the salami. And I would be left at home. Waiting.

Don't say it. Don't cling. If you do, they can't breathe.

Reaching for my wine glass I took a big mouthful and swallowed away the ghost of a lump.

Fake It

One day I heard a woman on the radio talking about social media and 'the virtual self'. She described how people use Facebook and Twitter, posting photos and updates, comments and gags, to 'display themselves' to the world. The presenter asked her if she thought we were all 'tinkering with what we've put online in order to project the image of ourselves that we want to project'. The social media expert told him we're all 'sculpting ourselves' using the medium of digital data, creating 'virtual doppelgangers' out there in cyberspace in order to 'craft Brand Me'.

The radio program was all about The Future. The presenter spoke with a breathlessness usually reserved for Exciting Medical Breakthroughs or for Evidence of Life on Mars. But that's not so new, I told my radio, that 'crafting Brand Me' thing. Erving Goffman figured out fifty years ago that we're all trying to 'fake it till we make it'. I had discovered him in the library when I was researching shyness.

Goffman started his working life with the Canadian National

Film Board during the Second World War. One of the Board's earliest missions was to create government propaganda, including some 'morale-boosting theatrical shorts' called *Canada Carries On*. Goffman must have seen a lot of people carrying on for the camera back in those early years. A lot of people pretending to be something they weren't. A lot of strategic fakery. Later he became a sociologist and in 1950 he wrote a book in which he argued that we're all creating a kind of daily theatre out of our lives, applying the dramaturgical touch to our interactions with other humans.

In *The Presentation of Self in Everyday Life* Goffman described how every social interaction we have involves putting on a mask and playing a role. These performances are designed to influence how others ('the audience') think and feel about us. Sometimes we're sincere in our performance, he wrote, and sometimes we're cynical:

> The individual may attempt to induce the audience to judge him and the situation a particular way, and he may seek this judgment as an ultimate end in itself, and yet he may not completely believe that he deserves the valuation of self which he asks for, or that the impression of reality which he fosters is valid.

Reading the first few chapters of Goffman's book, I thought of Shy Sian metamorphosing into Professional Sian in that job interview for the ACF. Was she being sincere or cynical in there? Was she convinced by the version of herself that she was presenting to the interview panel? Or had her sincere belief in the greater cause (saving the world) enabled her to leapfrog any cynicism or self-doubt about her own performance?

About a month into the ACF job, the boss called me into his

office to tell me there had been a leak of radioactive material from a tailings dam in a Northern Territory uranium mine. He urgently needed a press release sent out. I had an hour.

I can still feel the wave of anxiety that crashed over me as I nodded and walked briskly back to my desk. I had never written a press release before. I had no idea where to start. But I had talked my way into this job, hadn't I? I'd put on the award-winning performance for the interview panel. I couldn't let the mask slip now.

Back at my desk I was finding it hard to breathe. After several long minutes I unobtrusively crossed the open plan office and opened a filing cabinet that had been used by my predecessor. Rifling through the drawers with trembling fingers, I found a file on Australian uranium mines. No press releases. Damn. But there was a contact number for a campaigner at the Northern Territory Environment Centre. I dialled the number and, putting on my best new Professional Sian voice, asked this invisible stranger for a 'briefing'.

My memory of the rest of the performance has faded. The press release must have gone out. The stranger at the end of the phone later became one of my closest confidantes, gratitude morphing into friendship yet again. All I remember now is the scene where the woman playing the part of the environment campaigner realises she's a fake. And yet she got away with it. The performance was working.

But why on earth had it seemed so vital to maintain the illusion of a self-confident professional persona that day? Why hadn't I just said to the boss, 'You know what, I've never actually written a press release before and I could do with some help'? Erving Goffman has an answer for this one too:

Performers may even attempt to give the impression that their present poise and proficiency are something they have always had and that they have never had to fumble their way through a learning period. In all of this the performer may receive tacit assistance from the establishment in which he is to perform.

Tacit assistance. So my 'audience' of employers *wanted* me to pretend to know what I was doing? If Goffman was right, in order to keep the job I probably didn't have any choice except faking it till I made it.

Years later when I first heard the term 'Impostor Syndrome' I knew immediately what 'a psychological phenomenon in which competent people find it impossible to believe in their own competence' felt like. Tom had his own label for it. He called it 'the pretendies' and we had compared notes on those moments when you suddenly and inexplicably lose faith in your ability to carry off the things you're meant to be competent to do, like writing anything of any interest to anyone ever again, for example. And yet we both continued to write.

People had often told me that I seemed to be a very calm person. A long time ago a poet I desperately wanted (but never came close to getting) described me as 'inaccessible, like a kind of mystic'. More recently the wife of Tom's manager had said to me 'you're so still, you're like a sphinx'. At the time I was seated next to her at a dinner table full of people who were strangers to me, fighting a sandstorm of social anxiety that threatened to suck me under the table.

Erving Goffman would have been right onto me. 'Perhaps the focus of the dramaturgical discipline is to be found in the management of one's face and voice. Here is the crucial test of one's ability as a performer. Actual affective response must be concealed and an appropriate affective response must be displayed.' Hence my fake air of calm. In fact it was when I appeared most Zen that my 'actual affective response' was off the Richter scale. Why had I always believed that my anxiety had to be hidden from the world? After some more ferreting around in the library I discovered that, about five years ago, Goffman's theory about social interactions as a series of staged identity performances by human 'actors' had been picked up by an English sociologist called Dr Susie Scott and applied specifically to shyness. And Dr Scott was *not* happy.

'What is it about our culture that demands that we pretend to be poised, skilled and assertive in our dealings with others, and what happens to those who appear to deviate from this norm?' she asked. 'Indeed, we might enquire as to what extent any of us are "really" like this underneath, and why we have this need to maintain the illusion of competence.'

You mean everyone else is faking it too? Then why do I usually feel like I'm the only person who doesn't know what they're doing in social situations? In *Shyness and Society: The Illusion of Competence* Dr Scott wrote:

> The shy person is extremely concerned about the risk of making a faux pas and exposing what they see as secret flaws in their characters, most notably their perceived lack of social skills. At the same time, shy people report feeling as if everybody else seems to know the unspoken rules of interaction and thus are able to provide a more poised, socially competent performance. This feeling of relative incompetence is central to the experience of shyness.

If only Susie Scott had been teaching sociology at my London school in 1979. She could have explained to me why I was spending lunchtimes hiding in the library instead of flirting in the schoolyard. I would have had the answer to this question, though: 'How might shy actors devise strategies to help them "pass" in social situations?' My hand would have shot up and waved madly from the front of the classroom.

That's what the sphinx's mask is for, Dr Scott. That's what my invisible professional cloaks have been for, the ones that allowed me to stop being *just me* and instead transform myself into a representative of something much larger and more powerful. That's what the protective initials were for: ACF campaigner, ACTU community artist, ABC broadcaster, RMIT lecturer. And that's why it made perfect sense to me that so many success-ful actors described themselves as shy. They could spend their working lives hiding behind the characters they were playing.

I remembered reading a magazine profile in which shy Oscar-winner Judy Davis talked about the 'pathetic subterfuges' she employed to avoid dealing with people. She explained how she would hide beneath a floppy hat and flourish a notepad and pen—'these ridiculous props', she called them—so she wouldn't have to talk to strangers at her children's school sports events. 'It's pathetic that an adult would behave like this,' Davis berated herself. But why did Judy Davis feel the need to berate herself? Why was she ashamed of her shyness? Why was I? Dr Scott had a theory about this, too:

> Shy people are intensely aware that this is a negotiated social order and that by being withdrawn and reticent they might be seen as failing to pull their weight. Their behaviour can variously be normalised, sanctioned as social deviance, or pathologised as a mental disorder... The idea that shyness is a personal affliction that holds us back from social life is one so widely accepted that

it seems like common sense...And yet it is these very taken for granted, common sense statements about 'what everyone knows' that exert a subtle and complicit form of control over social behaviour.

But according to the psychiatric manuals, Dr Scott, if your shyness is so bad you can't leave the house then it *is* a mental disorder. Even though I had almost always been able to make myself leave the house in spite of it, shyness *had* felt like an affliction that had held me back, and not one imposed from the outside but from inside my own anxious brain. It was hard to believe that Judy Davis and I were passive victims of a hegemonic shyness-hating culture. Dr Scott was adamant.

> The shy may represent one of many groups of modern-day folk-devils about whom there is a moral panic... The dominant message...is that non-shyness is normal and acceptable while shyness is deviant and undesirable, carrying with it the risk of social exclusion...It is time to stop berating shy people for their presumed misanthropy.

Folk-devils? Moral panic? Good grief! Where were the indignant talkback callers, the shock jocks foaming at the mouth about the threat to the civil order from deviant shy folk? Socially anxious people like me weren't being tossed in village ponds to see if we would sink or swim.

And yet hadn't I already confessed my impatience with other shy people and my desire for them to conquer their fears? Maybe I had been unconsciously reflecting the shyness-hating values of the exhibitionist, competitive, extrovert-worshipping society in which I had been raised.

Or maybe I just didn't want to be battling this shameful thing alone.

'The misperception of shyness as rudeness or aloofness is one that "plagues" shy people,' Susie Scott continued, 'but their accounts suggest that they actually feel the complete opposite way about social life.' Aloofness, yes, I had been accused of that. Selfishness, that was another interpretation I'd been offered—we shy people are not prepared to 'pull our weight'. I'd even had one socially confident person tell me she thought shy behaviour was a form of emotional manipulation, a strategy for making other people feel sorry for us in order to get what we want from them.

'Wanting desperately to participate but feeling ill-equipped to do so, the shy recount feelings of frustrated sociability, alienation and exclusion,' wrote Susie Scott. That's the essential difference between shyness and introversion, I thought, right there. As Margot had explained, introverts are not necessarily unhappy being alone. I, on the other hand, had often felt an urgent desire for human company, for intense connection with others, but had had to fight my way through a thicket of fears to find those things. The pattern of behaviour that had begun all those years ago with my childhood friend Sally, a reluctance to visit anyone unless I had received a clear invitation, had continued to the present day. Most of the time social spontaneity was out of the question. Stupid and self-limiting, but so deeply ingrained I couldn't seem to break out of it.

An Apology

Actually I tell a lie. Shock jocks in Australia *had* been foaming at the mouth about the threat to the civil order from deviant shy folk. From one shy woman, anyway.

On my computer desktop there was a newspaper photo I had downloaded from the web. In the background of the photo was a higgledy-piggedly line of hand-painted banners and placards. On one of the banners a black cartoon witch was perched on a black cartoon broomstick and surrounded by black stencilled words in aggressive caps: DITCH THE WITCH. Beside this placard there was a poster with more black text, this time in curly lettering hand-drawn over the top of leaping orange flames that looked like they'd used up a big box of someone's Derwents: JULIAR... BOB BROWN'S BITCH. The signs were being held aloft by a smiling crowd of my fellow Australians and their target was the nation's first female prime minister, Julia Gillard.

After Ms Gillard took over her party's leadership about a year before this photo was taken, a small clutch of male shock-jocks began a campaign of unprecedented public vitriol against the

PM. Their listeners responded by holding a series of public rallies at which the banners had become progressively more lurid. The leader of the opposition attended a few of these rallies, and in the photo saved to my computer his white business shirt and shiny orange tie were perfectly colour-matched to the leaping flames of hell on the banner behind him.

In the midst of this flurry of protests the then prime minister gave a speech at a Press Club luncheon during which, it was reported, she described herself as having been a 'shy girl' when she was young. Not just described, but 'tearfully confessed', according to some journalists. Reading the prurient, patronising headlines, I found myself squirming with a mixture of empathy and disapproval. *Why did you let them see you cry? Why admit this publicly? What good could possibly come of it?*

I knew a bit about politics. I had an honours degree in the stuff. And now I knew quite a lot about shyness. My hand was waving hard from the front row of the classroom. I would have my say.

So I sat down and wrote a cool, clinical opinion piece for the newspapers, arguing that the PM's admission of shyness had been a political mistake. Public perceptions of shyness are linked with a Rubik's cube of negative stereotypes, I argued, including self-consciousness, self-pity, emotional withdrawal, social awkwardness and a lack of assertiveness. Publicly ascribing these qualities to one's own personality is no way to win friends or influence people. After all, who wants to vote for an unassertive leader?

Confessing to shyness can often provoke bullying rather than sympathy, I added, and besides, the fact that the prime minister didn't behave in public like a stereotypical shy person meant she risked confirming the shock jocks' assertions that she wasn't an honest person—that she was 'Ju-liar'.

Perhaps the biggest problem for our shy prime minister, I continued, was her gender. Many of the attributes ascribed to shyness have been associated with stereotypically female behaviours. Men are assertive, women are timid. Men speak, women listen. Men stick to their guns, women are easily swayed by their emotions—or so the myth goes. Most female political leaders are forced to counter these stereotypes throughout their careers or risk being dismissed as unfit to lead. With that one small 's' word, our PM would potentially confirm the prejudices of those who were already suspicious of her simply because she's a woman.

The piece was published and I felt the usual self-congratulatory rush when I read my by-line on the opinion page. In the days following its publication, though, I began to feel less and less like congratulating myself. My email inbox was soon overflowing with readers' responses.

> Sian, when I read your article regarding Julia Gillard's comments about her shyness I thought you must be one of those right-leaning journalists who have been lining up ever since Julia became prime minister to having a go at kicking her down until she gave up.

> Dear Ms Prior, I read your article in today's newspaper. What can I say? Great effort at sinking the slipper. You sound like the thinking person's shock jock. Ever considered a talk-back career?

> Dear Sian, re. your piece in the paper today. Seems Gillard's either a liar or weak. I guess shy people can't get a break, eh? Seeing as you describe yourself as shy, makes me wonder about your website. Are you weak or a liar too? If either, why should we take any notice

of you, your blog site or your pop-psychology effort in the *Age*? What are your qualifications to write the rubbish you wrote?

I felt sick. My so-called clinical political analysis had turned out to be just another hand-painted placard of insults waving in the wind. *All writers must first charm, then betray*, it said on a card I had pinned over my desk. In trying to show off my newfound knowledge about shyness it seemed I had committed an act of public betrayal.

Like me, the prime minister had found her voice (and maybe an escape from her shyness) through student political activism. Unlike me, she had had the guts to stick at it. I didn't agree with all of her policies but I admired her willingness to stand up to the entrenched misogyny of Australian party politics. As I forced myself to read through all the angry email responses, two ideas collided in my mind...

1. Shyness is a form of weakness (deep down, I had always believed this)
2. Women are weaker than men (deep down, I had never believed this)

...and produced a third idea:

3. My very clever opinion piece wasn't about the prime minister. It was about me. And maybe it was another piece in the puzzle.

I remembered my paralysis as the boys from my primary school disappeared down the end of our driveway, leaving the orange tree stripped of its fruit, me stripped of my voice. I remembered the cold wet remnants of fear in my gut, fear that they wouldn't like me, fear that if I said anything about the naked tree they would never come back. I remembered how, even way back then, I felt ashamed of my weakness, my silence, my need for their approval.

And I remembered the relief of getting to university and discovering that this weakness, this shame, this need for male approbation, had a cure. It was called feminism and I embraced it like a drowner with a lifebuoy.

My battle against shyness hadn't just been a campaign of self-improvement. Somewhere along the line it had got tangled up with my understanding that, as a woman, I would have to fight against the assumption that I was inevitably weaker than men and therefore undeserving of an equal voice. I couldn't be a shy feminist; it would be an oxymoron. And I would be a feminist. So I would have to stop being shy.

Maybe the shock jocks had been foaming at the mouth not because Julia Gillard was shy, but because she was a woman refusing to behave like a weak person, and that represented more of a threat to their sense of civil order than an entire army of shy people.

It turns out I was not the only opportunistic journalist who leapt on the Shy Julia story that week. In the days after her speech the airwaves were full of conversations with social anxiety experts and all the radio hosts were inviting their listeners to ring up and talk about shyness. I started taking notes, looking for evidence.

'Maude' rang in to report that, although she felt her shyness was a negative, she knew that her friends and colleagues respected the fact that she was 'a quiet one'. No social stigma to report there—just the usual anxious self-criticism.

But then talkback caller 'Emma' described how she was sent off to do an assertiveness course for her shyness, where she was told that 'to be self-conscious is selfish'.

And 'Bill' informed the listeners that he 'sometimes perceived shy people as having a lack of generosity of spirit, an unwillingness to get involved...they're a bit like people lying down in shopping malls to test if someone will stop'. Weak self-centred people, Bill, looking for sympathy.

Random talkback callers do not make a representative sample, but there seemed to be plenty of anecdotal evidence to support Susie Scott's theory that shyness is seen as a form of anti-social deviance. And to support my instinct that the prime minister would be judged poorly for her admission of shyness. I was right back where I had started.

Three years after she first became the prime minister, Julia Gillard was replaced by the man she had deposed to get the job. The day after her colleagues booted her out, a political commentator wrote in the *Guardian* newspaper about the:

> ...public perception that Gillard's prime ministerial identity was a protean thing, never entirely convincing, never entirely stable. Was she the 'real Julia' or something else?...She was intensely private, contained, reserved—stubbornly enigmatic and withholding for a person so long in the public spotlight. She rationed appearances by her best self.

It all sounded so horribly familiar.

She was a blusher, our first female prime minister. Careful make-up had kept her face looking creamy pale on my television screen night after night, but I had seen the treacherous colour creeping up her neck. I could feel that heat, sense the effort it cost her to keep the cool professional façade in place. She was one of my people.

Darwin's Blushes

One hundred and sixty-five years ago Mr Charles Darwin sat down at his desk to make some notes about shyness. He was planning a new book, *The Expression of the Emotions in Man and Animal*, and had been sending questionnaires all over the world to physicians and scientists who he thought might be able to help him with his investigations.

When he sat down to write, though, it was the expression of the emotions in the bodies of women that seemed to be of most interest to Mr Darwin. In particular, he wrote, he was 'desirous to learn how far down the body blushes extend'. Darwin reported that his friend Sir James Paget had found 'with women who blush intensely on the face, ears, and nape of neck, the blush does not commonly extend any lower down the body...'

Sir James had further advised that 'it is rare to see it as low down as the collar-bones and shoulder-blades; and he has never himself seen a single instance in which it extended below the upper part of the chest.' Sir James had been watching blushes both come and go.

Blushes sometimes die away downwards, not gradually and insensibly, but by irregular ruddy blotches. In most cases the face, ears and neck are the sole parts which redden; but many persons, whilst blushing intensely, feel that their whole bodies grow hot and tingle; and this shows that the entire surface must be in some manner affected.

Darwin's observant friend seems to have had quite an impact on the ladies.

Sir James Paget, whilst examining the spine of a girl, was struck at her singular manner of blushing; a big splash of red appeared first on one cheek, and then other splashes, variously scattered over the face and neck. He subsequently asked the mother whether her daughter always blushed in this peculiar manner; and was answered, 'Yes, she takes after me.' Sir J. Paget then perceived that by asking this question he had caused the mother to blush; and she exhibited the same peculiarity as her daughter.

Genes will out. Mr Darwin shows us that.

A certain Dr Browne offered Mr Darwin some intimate observations from within an insane asylum. A woman suffering from epilepsy was, according to Dr Browne, 'much agitated and tremulous'. Dr Browne took it upon himself to unfasten the collar of her chemise 'in order to examine the state of her lungs; and then a brilliant blush rushed over her chest, in an arched line over the upper third of each breast, and extended downwards between the breasts nearly to the ensiform cartilage of the sternum'.

'The foregoing facts show,' Mr Darwin concluded, 'that, as a general rule, with English women, blushing does not extend beneath the neck and upper part of the chest.' But what of the other races, Mr Darwin?

Fortunately the scientist knew some observant chaps in far-flung parts of the globe and they had kindly been filling out questionnaires for him too. 'Mr Swinhoe has seen the Chinese blushing, but he thinks it is rare; yet they have the expression "to redden with shame",' wrote Darwin. 'Mr Geach informs me that the Chinese settled in Malacca and the native Malays of the interior both blush. Some of these people go nearly naked, and he particularly attended to the downward extension of the blush.'

The intrepid Mr Forster clearly enjoyed doing the research for his eminent friend, reporting with enthusiasm that 'you may easily distinguish a spreading blush on the cheeks of the fairest women in Tahiti'. Furthermore, Darwin wrote, 'a perfectly characterised albino negress...showed a faint tinge of crimson on her cheeks when she exhibited herself naked.' The strategic employment of the Male Gaze in pursuit of scientific truth: now that's fieldwork.

Darwin's report is so full of lovingly detailed descriptions of the female body it is hard not to read them now as a kind of genteel pornography. But they were merely a prelude to a lengthy dissertation on shyness, shame and modesty, 'the mental states which induce blushing'. And Darwin was right onto those tandem torments of social anxiety: self-consciousness and fear of negative evaluation.

> It is not the simple act of reflecting on our own appearance, but the thinking what others think of us, which excites a blush...Shyness seems to depend on sensitiveness to the opinion, whether good or bad, of others, more especially with respect to external appearance.

Darwin's shyness chapter includes a tender description of his two-year-old son, who exhibited signs of the 'condition' when Darwin returned from a week-long absence. Darwin gently exhorts his readers not to reprimand children for shyness in grappling with the scrutiny of 'the unmerciful spectator'. Perhaps the boy had inherited his father's shyness. Perhaps, like me, Mr Darwin was conducting an investigation of his own temperament. Perhaps he was trying to figure out why such a torturous genetic inheritance persisted, whether there was any evolutionary benefit involved.

I stopped reading Darwin's chapter for a moment and opened up a transcript of my interview with Professor Ron. This had come up, I recalled, when I had questioned him about why shy people were so afraid of negative evaluation.

PROFESSOR RON: Some people talk about it as an evolutionary thing, in terms of affiliation and keeping the group together—the idea that perhaps it's good for some creatures within a species to be more socially withdrawn than others. If everyone was equally outgoing then you would have a lot of aggression within the species. But if you've got some who are happy being down the bottom of the pack and others who are the more dominant ones, it's protective. The shy person is not going to get beaten up by the leader because they'll do what the leader says and the leader will protect them, as opposed to the more aggressive ones who might get kicked out of the group.

I certainly didn't want to risk being kicked out of any group, but 'down the bottom of the pack' was never a place I had wanted to be. No wonder I had been fighting this thing so hard.

Googling shyness + evolution, I found a recent article in *New Scientist* about how evolutionary theory had been applied to the study of shyness in the late twentieth century.

Turns out humans are not the only creatures born somewhere on the 'shy–bold' spectrum. One researcher discovered that some salamanders are shyer than other salamanders, and the shy ones are better at avoiding being gobbled up by predators than the bold ones. On the other hand, the bold ones eat more and grow faster, which helps them to stay in the evolutionary race. Among bird species, the article reported, boldness was manifest as a personality trait called 'exploration'. Again, there were evolutionary costs and benefits to being an avian explorer. In some years the environment favoured the bold birds, in other years it favoured those who preferred to hide in the nearest nook or cranny. Both ends of the shyness spectrum were important for species survival.

I went back to Darwin.

> Shyness, as the derivation of the word indicates in several languages, is closely related to fear, yet it is distinct from fear in the ordinary sense. A shy man no doubt dreads the notice of strangers, but can hardly be said to be afraid of them, he may be as bold as a hero in battle, and yet have no self-confidence about trifles in the presence of strangers.

Bold as a hero, like my shy father.

This raised the question of etymology, which fortunately I could investigate without sending questionnaires around the globe and waiting for sailing ships to bring them home again. Google had the answers for me in half a second.

Webster's online dictionary reported that the English word *shy* was already in use by the twelfth century and that it came from the Middle English word *schey*. This word had come from the Old English *sceoh* which was akin to the Old High German word *sciuhen*. As Mr Darwin had reported, all these words referenced the idea of being afraid.

Were shy English-speaking people in the twelfth century just as afraid as we shy English-speaking folk in the twenty-first century? Presumably they mostly lived in small villages and encountered fewer strangers in their daily lives. On the other hand, stranger-danger was probably a rational response to that lawless century. Random robberies were rife. Protection money was regularly 'levied' from poor villagers and torture was commonplace. No blushing body part was safe from the noose, the chain, the stone, the iron or the adder. Maintaining a healthy fear of negative evaluation by those you didn't know was probably wise in those circumstances.

Another dictionary website reported that in the nineteenth century the word 'shy' took a strange swerve and was used colloquially to mean 'disreputable', possibly leading to the word 'shyster'. I briefly wondered if Shakespeare's fictional usurer Shylock had had anything to do with this transmutation but none of the dictionaries made the connection. One offered the advice, however, that the word 'shylock' was now being used to mean zipper or fly, 'as a security feature for your shy bits'.

Perhaps that's why Mr Darwin's ladies had been blushing so furiously. All those medical men staring at their shy bits, causing them to feel ashamed. Interesting, how the words 'shame' and 'shy' feel so similar in your mouth when you speak them out loud. I had always felt ashamed of my blushing shyness, but why?

Ferreting around in the library again I found a book called *Blush: Faces of Shame* by an Australian cultural theorist. Professor Elspeth Probyn was a shy blusher, too, often bewildered by her body's treacherous reactions, and she had decided to get to the bottom of it. In investigating why we're ashamed to admit to these feelings, Professor Probyn had found a way to 'positively re-frame' blushing and shame.

'Shame makes us quiver,' she wrote. 'Being shamed is not unlike being in love...The blush resonates with the first flush of desire...the skin feels raw.' I knew what she meant. I could still remember the quivering feelings of the early days of my relationship with Tom: the fluttering in my belly, the heat in my face, the hyper-acuity that engulfed my senses, as if I was permanently on the verge of a pleasurable migraine. Those feelings might have dulled a little over the years but they hadn't entirely gone away.

According to Professor Probyn, what we desire when we feel shame is 'positive evaluation' from others. 'If you're interested in and care about the interest of others, you spend much of your life blushing,' Elspeth Probyn wrote.

> Shame highlights different levels of interest (and) interest involves a desire for connection. At a basic level, it has to do with our longings for communication, touch, lines of entanglement and reciprocity...The things that make me feel ashamed have to do with a strong interest in being a good person.

Elspeth Probyn's book was an extended argument for the social utility of shame. Shame made us better people because, she wrote, 'shame brings the fear of abandonment by society, of being left to starve outside the boundaries of humankind'. If I hadn't cared as much about what other people thought about me, hadn't been so afraid of their 'negative evaluation', I probably wouldn't have spent so much time trying to be a Good Influence. Was this another difference between shy people, including shy extroverts like me, and introverts? Perhaps introverts didn't have as much invested in what others thought of them, and consequently didn't feel the same level of shame about their inability to behave like social butterflies.

Professor Probyn believed it was possible that 'shame involves an internalisation of an idealised other to which the self has failed to live up: the sense of shame is a reaction…to the consciousness of this loss'. Reading these words I remembered Magazine Woman and how she had haunted me, a flawless fictional female, my idealised other. These days people who worry about their flaws can pay a medical expert to tidy them up. If only there was a medical procedure you could have to remove the chronic embarrassment that accompanies shyness. Perhaps that's what the blushing female patients of Mr Darwin's medical colleagues were secretly hoping for too.

Virtual Self

I had started observing my writing students more closely, trying to figure out which ones were shy and which ones weren't. In each group there was the usual mix of willing speakers and near-silent listeners. I now understood, though, that the speech-to-silence ratio wasn't always the best indicator of who was grappling with social anxiety.

Many of them brought their laptops to class and one day as I was walking back to my desk I passed behind a pretty young woman who had been staring despondently at her computer screen for much of the class. She was usually the most talkative in the group but that day she had said very little. Glancing down I saw her face staring out from the glowing screen. She had the computer's camera trained on herself and was so engrossed by her mirror image, she didn't even notice me looking at her. I wondered if, in her mind's eye, she could see Magazine Woman standing behind her—if she was negotiating with the same fearful self-consciousness that had drawn me to the mirror when I was her age.

The quietest student in that group, another young woman, usually spent a lot of class time tapping on her keyboard. She was one of the more diligent ones and I had assumed she was taking notes. I'd been worried about her. She never seemed to mix with the other students in the cafe but spent the break alone in the classroom. She must be shy, I told myself. And lonely. One day, before the other students had returned to class, I asked her what she was writing. Coyly she turned the computer towards me and there, scrolling across the screen, was a conversation in text, a witty, flirtatious interaction between someone called Honeyman and my student, known to her correspondent as Cute 'n' Cuddly.

I should have been grumpy with her, flirting online instead of noting down my pearls of wisdom. Instead I was full of admiration. She's not lonely, I thought, and she's not unsociable. She's adaptive. The digital world has offered her a safe way to have the kind of flirtatious fun that extroverts take for granted.

I went looking for information about shyness and the internet. In a book called *Cyberspace Romance: The Psychology of Online Relationships* two social psychologists, Monica Whitty and Adrian Carr, had surveyed the latest research on how people used the internet to find new friends and to look for love.

According to one study, many shy people use online dating sites to 'overcome inhibitions that would normally have prevented them from attempting to initiate a relationship face to face'. Other researchers claimed that the visual anonymity of online communication and what they called the 'lack of co-presence—the physical isolation—of the communicators add to the interaction possibilities, and for some this is the "magic" of online relationships'. Was that the magic of invisibility that I had always longed for?

I thought about how Tom and I had emailed each other for months before we got together, enabling me to detour around the physical self-consciousness that usually got in my way when I was keen on someone. Whitty and Gavin should have interviewed us. We could have confirmed their findings that internet users feel less aware of 'being socially evaluated, which in turn allowed these individuals to reveal intimate details about themselves while maintaining distance and personal space'.

The ghost of Erving Goffman haunted this book, with many researchers talking about the different 'selves' we carry around with us. The one that interested me most was called the *true self,* a version of ourselves that includes characteristics that we would *like* to express but are not usually able to demonstrate to others. 'People who are lonely or are socially anxious in traditional face to face interaction settings (are) likely to feel better able to express their *true* self over the internet and so to develop close and meaningful relationships.'

The book used a metaphor for internet dating called 'bundling'. This was originally an American colonial practice in which a young woman would invite a suitor to go to bed with her, fully clothed, in her own home. In some cases there was even a board placed between their bodies to prevent any sexual contact. Bundling offered young people a chance to get to know each other in private but without any risk of 'inappropriate' contact.

Imagine it, the warm breath on your face, the shy confessions, the comforting layers of cotton and wool between your flesh and his. It sounded like my kind of courting. It also sounded like the kind of safe intimacy I had felt with only a computer screen between Tom and me.

In recent years some of my female friends had joined online

dating sites. At least one had since married a man she'd met online. The awkwardness that used to accompany admissions of internet dating had all but gone. But how did it work? I tried to sneak a look at one of the most popular sites but it required me to join up to get access. Feeling like a fraud, I set up an account for myself with a pseudonym and an alternative email address. After all, it wasn't as if I was actually looking for love. I had found it with Tom, in spades, and had no desire to muck it up with any untoward digital bundling.

Ignoring the advice on the dating website to post a photo of myself, I scrolled down to the section that required a brief self-description and wrote: 'I'm shy, are you?'

In the days that followed I was astonished by how many men responded to my one-line description. Some sent pro forma requests to get to know me better. Some even invested money in sending me sweet emails, confessing their own shyness. Once again I was full of admiration. These men were shy but determined not to be alone with it. I trawled through their photos and profiles: men on fishing boats, men holding hands with their smiling children, men who looked like amputees because they'd cropped a photo of themselves with one arm around the shoulders of some long-gone woman. So much loneliness. So much hope. Such risk of rejection.

After a couple of weeks I couldn't stand my own fakery and deleted the profile.

I was retrospectively envious. If only this option had been available when I was younger. My students could socialise while sitting alone in their bedroom in front of a screen. They could join invisible communities of people who shared their own obscure interests. They could create semi-fictional characters to inhabit while conversing with other possibly semi-fictional young folk.

They could guide digital avatars of themselves around imaginary worlds, cartoon characters who were possibly better dressed, better looking and more socially skilled than their creators.

During my own adolescence there were no PCs, no emails, no Facebook and no Second Life. Most of my vicarious experience of the world came from books, and as a teenager I had spent many weekends lying under the glare of a bedside lamp, avoiding new, interesting and unpredictable social interactions in order to read about them.

Eventually, though, Professional Sian had taken me to many of the places I would have lacked the courage to go on my own. She was my avatar: my tool for self-reinvention, the version of myself who had allowed me to make it up as I went along. Some of the time, anyway.

The Wireless

When it came to work, sometimes I had pushed myself into the professional world and sometimes the professional world had come calling. The medium of radio had sought me out like an extroverted new friend. Working as an environment campaigner I had always loved doing radio interviews: invisible me, hiding behind my world-saving persona, using my voice, preaching my cause—the microphone drew me in like a bee to a flower.

Saving the world had proven to be too much for one person: after three years of intense campaigning I needed a break. Besides, staying on top of the maths of climate change and ozone depletion, all those terrifying parts per million, was slowly crushing the words and music out of me. I spent a year doing a community arts traineeship with the trade union movement, organising concerts in workplaces and starting up the trade union choir (aka Comrade Choir Mistress). Just as the traineeship was about to end, a team of community radio broadcasters offered me a job. They made current affairs programs about all those things that I still thought were Wrong With The Planet. It sounded perfect. So there I was, saving the world again, one radio program at a time.

It turned out that radio reporting was a dream job for a shy, opinionated, helpful show-off:

- Meet new and interesting people every week.
- Interview them within a limited time frame, avoiding the need for small talk.
- Send them away again.

After a couple of years in community radio I did my impersonation of a successful job candidate again and landed a gig as a reporter on a daily arts program at the ABC, an even more perfect job for a shy, opinionated, arty show-off. What could possibly be more interesting than interviewing:

- A linguist who had translated Hamlet's 'to be or not to be' speech into Klingon
- A digital artist who created photos of a fashion model holding a mouse that had a genetically engineered human ear growing on its back
- A theatre director who produced a show in which audience members were offered fellatio on stage
- A shy writer whose memoir described her life as a heroin-addicted prostitute working in brothels under a protective professional pseudonym
- A photographer who superimposed images of Elvis Presley's face onto black and white photos of heroes of the Russian Revolution (aka Comrade Elvis)
- A composer who wrote a chamber opera about Australian surf lifesavers
- A songwriter called Tom who, many years later, would send me an email that changed everything.

For half a decade Professional Sian was happier than she had ever been before, travelling around the country visiting arts festivals, interviewing humans about the sublime and ridiculous products of their imaginations. Being an arts critic allowed me to feel helpful, too. I could give an artist *pos re* when their work was good, praising them in front of an invisible audience of radio listeners, and offer some gentle *neg re* when it wasn't. Being a Good Influence on the national culture.

I developed a drug-like dependence on the hormone highs that came from regular doses of performance anxiety. In the hours leading up to the moment when the microphone was switched on and my voice went to air, I would invariably endure a racing heart, a dry mouth and a churning gut. Classic fight-or-flight response, the neuroscientists would say. The body priming itself for danger with a flood of adrenaline and noradrenaline. Once I started speaking, though, my words usually flowed in a perfectly logical order. And when the microphone was turned off I would float back down the corridor to my office in a state of elation. This stuff was addictive. It was worth fighting the fear for the pleasure that came afterwards. Had that been a factor in my battles with social anxiety? Had I become addicted to post-exposure therapy highs?

Eventually I was asked to present my own weekly arts program on the radio. The *what ifs* kicked in immediately. *What if* the listeners didn't like me? *What if* I choked on air? In spite of my anxiety (or perhaps because of it) I couldn't refuse. There was no other job I would rather be doing.

Sometimes being a studio presenter felt like being in a tour bus at a free-range zoo. Safe inside my sealed capsule I could observe and discuss the fascinating habits of homo sapiens without any risk to life and limb. Although I was interacting with the people I interviewed, we were in a highly controlled environment. My audience couldn't see me and I couldn't see them, so it was impossible to tell if they were evaluating me positively or negatively: I could be a confident, articulate, disembodied voice.

At times that disembodiment felt quite literal. Sometimes I would meet people in social situations years after Professional Sian had interviewed them on the radio. Shy Sian would squint and duck her head in the usual awkward way, not realising until they mentioned it that we had met before. The person who'd spoken to all those strangers on the wireless wasn't the same person who was now shaking hands with them.

Even after I moved into arts journalism my youthful list of Things Wrong With The World wasn't forgotten. When, just occasionally, those things were righted, I wanted to be there to celebrate. After East Timor finally gained its independence from Indonesia early in the new millennium I packed my recording equipment and flew to the capital, Dili, to find some stories to tell.

I wandered the streets of the burnt-out capital, meeting with strangers in noisy roadside cafes, plying them with questions about the ecotourism potential of this reef-fringed island. I accepted lifts from strangers to the far end of the island where I sat on other strangers' porches, their roosters pecking around my feet, and interviewed them about national language policies. I drank gin and tonics with yet more strangers in beachside bars and asked them about the rehabilitation of violent prisoners in East Timor's overflowing jails. I recorded interviews with the freedom-fighter-turned-president about how he planned to turn this nation of torture victims into a utopian model of civil society. I consulted with the foreign minister (a Nobel Peace

Prize-winning helpful person) about the idea of helping him write his autobiography. Once again I was determined to be a Good Influence and, in the guise of Professional Sian, I could be virtually fearless.

On Entomology

Whenever Tom went away for work I tried to fill the gap with social events. Theatre dates, book club, clothes-swap nights, DVD marathons: my diary was a hieroglyphic mess. Anything to distract me from missing Tom. 'You're such a social butterfly,' one friend said to me at the end of a particularly manic week.

Now there's an ambiguous term. Compliment or insult? Aren't social butterflies the people whose attention you can never hang on to because as soon as their interest wanes they're fluttering off to the next thing? At the very least the metaphor implies a lightness of touch. Whereas in the company of people I didn't know very well, I usually felt more like a beached walrus.

Butterflies in the stomach, of course, I knew about; but it wasn't until recently that I had begun to understand the treacherous connection between entomology and gastroenterology.

On a social anxiety website I found a notice about a public talk on something called the brain-gut axis. The guest speaker was an Australian clinical psychologist, Dr Simon Knowles, who worked with people suffering from chronic illnesses of the gastro-intestinal system. Dr Knowles began his talk by describing several case studies of women who had consulted him about their misbehaving bowels. He had assigned them a series of pseudonyms.

> Ms Overwhelmed is a perfectionist, a worrier, and highly sensitive to stress. She spends a lot of time focusing on 'shoulds' like 'I should never make a mistake' and telling herself 'if I make a mistake I must be stupid'. She has had gut problems for years but they got a lot worse after she had a relationship break-up.
>
> Then there is 'Ms Work Pride', a habitual catastrophiser who had been to see a GP, a gastroenterologist, a dietician *and* a psychologist to try and sort out her digestive problems. She had also had investigative surgery, all with no benefit. Like ninety per cent of people with these gastro-intestinal problems, the women I've described were very high functioning. In other words smart, and very anxious.

What pseudonym might Dr Knowles invent for me? How about 'Ms Butterflies'? I could practically write the case study notes for him myself.

> Ms Butterflies first noticed her symptoms when she was backpacking around Europe in her early twenties. Her digestive system was like a runaway train and she had pains and bloating in her belly. Over the ensuing years she found that her symptoms worsened when her work involved public performances and stressful deadlines, or when her relationships were going badly. She consulted her GP. The GP sent her to a gastroenterologist. The gastroenterologist advised her to have a colonoscopy. No cause was discovered with this investigation.

Next she underwent a gastroscopy. Again, no luck. Meanwhile Ms Butterflies was finding that more and more different types of food could set off her distressing symptoms.

She consulted a Chinese doctor. The Chinese doctor persuaded her to spend a lot of time boiling up herbs to produce a brown liquid that tasted like sump oil. The sump oil had no appreciable impact on her guts. She consulted a naturopath. The naturopath prescribed her a beanbag's worth of tiny white pills, but to no avail. She tried acupuncture. This made her scalp tingle as if she had butterflies in her brain. It did nothing to prevent the butterflies in her stomach carrying on like a swarm of angry bees. So back she went to the gastroenterologist, who arranged to have her tested for coeliac disease and fructose intolerance. The test results were inconclusive. Her symptoms, however, were real. Eating often made her feel wretched.

According to Dr Knowles, Ms Butterflies' symptoms were probably the direct result of anxiety. Most of his anxious Ms's were suffering from IBS, or irritable bowel syndrome, an inflammatory bowel disease caused by an interaction between the gut's nervous system and the brain. The IBS symptoms he described exactly mirrored my digestive torments, including butterflies in the tummy, the result of 'the gut reacting in a protective, survival response'. Clicking through his Power Point presentation, Dr Knowles highlighted a list of the factors associated with IBS:

1. *Genetic predisposition* (Ms Butterflies remembered her grandfather Lloyd sitting up to dinner at exactly the same time every evening, fingers drumming nervously on the dining table, his meals a limited rotation of easy-to-digest

dishes invariably chased down by an overripe banana—she could never throw out one of these flaccid specimens without thinking of him.)

2. *Visceral hypersensitivity* (Ms Butterflies thought she knew what hypersensitive meant—it had been part of the family psych talk—but this sounded more clinical: she made a note to look it up later.)

3. *Psychosocial factors* (Ms Butterflies listened to the psychologist's description of the stress-prone, perfectionist personality type most vulnerable to IBS and recognised herself as if in a mirror.)

4. *Early family environment* (Ms Butterflies wondered about those months following her father's death and whether the sudden flood of grief and anxiety in her mother could have somehow stimulated a permanent, protective survival response in her infant digestive system.)

'You could think of the gut as being like a second brain,' Dr Knowles continued. 'Two thirds of IBS patients have a psychiatric disorder such as generalised anxiety, social anxiety and panic disorder. All of those can be accompanied by nausea, muscle tension and abdominal distress because anxiety leads to an over-activation of the fight-or-flight response.'

It was disconcerting hearing my anxiety described as a psychiatric disorder. But when I recalled my panicked flight from that birthday party, guts churning like a washing machine, the evidence was hard to deny.

The good news, Dr Knowles reported, was that effective treatment techniques are available for anxiety-induced IBS, including 'Breathing, Relaxation, Mindfulness and Acceptance, Exercise, Meditation, Yoga and Gut-Focused Hypnotherapy'. That last one made me giggle. I pictured a dark-eyed hypnotherapist with a slow-swinging fob watch staring soulfully at my belly button and intoning 'you're getting sleepy' in a deep baritone.

I couldn't help wondering about another tummy metaphor and how it might relate to the brain-gut axis. Dr Knowles had explained what goes wrong in your guts when you're feeling fearful. Why, then, did we often describe courageous people as gutsy? Were they the ones who were willing to ignore the warnings coming from their stomachs and carry on regardless? Or the ones whose bellies knew no fear?

Perhaps the people I had encountered on Professor Ron's *Overcoming Social Phobia* video—handsome Jon, laughing Lisa, sad Eric—were the courageous ones. Having a casual chat at the supermarket checkout or going to the local dance may have been intensely frightening for them, but somehow they had managed to do those things in spite of the dire warnings from their guts.

If I had spent my life avoiding every situation that made me feel anxious, perhaps I would still have a perfectly functioning digestive system. No foods off the menu, no Chinese sump-oil concoctions or naturopathic beanbag fillers. I could have sailed quietly through my life as a social isolate, living vicariously through the characters in my favourite novels. Instead I had pushed myself over a million small cliffs. My guts had paid the price.

Which Poison?

Before I met Andre, Valium was just a pop-culture cliché to me. Technicolor images of 1950s housewives obsessively wiping their white cliffs of cleanliness and going crazy with boredom. 'Mother's Little Helper': the pill prescribed for women who actually needed a strong dose of second-wave feminism. Before Andre I had never encountered it as a medication for a severe anxiety disorder and, judging from its impact on his life, it wasn't exactly a miracle cure. It had only caused his world to shrink further.

Perhaps that's why I never considered taking anti-anxiety drugs for my shyness. They didn't seem to work. Or perhaps I never really thought of myself as ill and in need of medication. I just thought I needed to work a bit harder to control my neurotic fears. Me and half a million other Australians.

When I was tracking down Professor Ron I found a website for the Macquarie University Anxiety Research Unit where he worked. 'Over 400,000 adult Australians suffer from significant social anxiety problems each year,' the website informed me, but 'only a small number of sufferers seek help'. As a result, 'social anxiety can be life-long if not treated effectively and can also lead to depression and alcohol abuse'. I remembered the birthday party in the art gallery and my flight to the safety of the car. If I hadn't been avoiding alcohol that night, perhaps I would have been able to sedate myself out of my state of panic. And perhaps this whole quest to get to the bottom of my shyness would never have begun.

Reasons why I love a glass of wine (or three):

- the feel of the cool strong glass in my hot trembling hand, liquid sand alchemised into solid clarity
- the first few sips of tart sweetness and the way they slide down the back of my throat, easing the tightness in there
- the next few sips, tartness gone, nothing but sweetness now, and the way they gently euthanise the butterflies in my belly
- the first few sips of the second glass, firmly clasped in my cool strong hand, and the way they lengthen my sentences, widen my smile
- the next few sips going down my relaxed throat and the way they meet the laughter on its way up
- the last dregs of the second glass, surely the best glass of wine I have *ever* tasted, at this, the best party I have been to in *years*
- the first few sips of the third glass and the way my hips have begun swaying ever-so-slightly, waiting for just the right music to come on
- the next few sips of the third glass and the way it doesn't seem to matter if my sentences don't quite have endings or, um, you know, that thing...

– the last few sips of the third glass—gone so soon?—and the
way I can stop talking now and just smile benignly at the
lovely, fuzzy people having a lovely, fuzzy time all around me.

Alcohol works a treat for shyness, as some anonymous wag in
cyberspace has attested:

Subject: Fw: Important Advice for all Women

Do you suffer from shyness?
Do you sometimes wish you were more assertive?
Do you have feelings of inadequacy?

If you answered yes to any of these questions, ask your
doctor or pharmacist about **Sauvignon Blanc**. It can help
ease you out of your shyness and let you tell the world that
you're ready and willing to do just about anything.

You will notice the benefits of **Sauvignon Blanc** almost
immediately and, with a regimen of regular doses,
shyness and awkwardness will be a thing of the past.
Stop hiding and start living. Side effects may include
dizziness, nausea, vomiting, incarceration, erotic
lustfulness, loss of motor control, loss of clothing,
loss of money, loss of virginity, delusions of grandeur,
table dancing, headache, dehydration, dry mouth, and a
desire to sing Karaoke and play all-night rounds of Strip
Poker, Truth Or Dare and Naked Twister.

Christopher Lane would definitely *not* have been amused by
this. In 2007 the English journalist wrote a book entitled
Shyness: How Normal Behaviour Became a Sickness, in which
he set out to prove that shyness had been deliberately patholo-
gised by a small but influential group of American psychiatrists
working hand in glove with the multinational pharmaceutical
industry. 'Shyness isn't just shyness anymore,' Lane wrote.

It's a disease (with) a variety of over-wrought names, including 'social anxiety' and 'avoidant personality disorder', afflictions said to trouble millions...And since the early 1990s, when (it was) agreed that powerful psychotropic drugs were suitable ways of treating these conditions, countless Americans and Britons have daily swallowed large doses of Paxil, Prozac, Zoloft and other pills for routine emotions that experts now consider medical conditions.

Lane argued that we have dramatically narrowed our conception of healthy behaviour. Our 'quirks and eccentricities' have now become problems that we fear and that we expect drugs to fix. It was all part of a pervasive cultural push towards mood brightening, and the consequence was 'a vast, perhaps unrecoverable, loss of emotional range, an impoverishment of human experience'.

Reading Christopher Lane's elegant, well-researched rant, I wondered again why I had never asked a doctor for some pills to muffle my anxious *what if*s. It's not as though I had a blanket prejudice against the use of drugs to treat psychological problems. I had several friends whose lives would have been almost intolerable without antidepressants. One of them had *literally* found life with depression intolerable and had opted instead for a snaking hose attached to a car exhaust. I had wished, hopelessly and retrospectively, that some smart doctor had thrust a prescription at him before it was too late.

Maybe, for him, anxiety had been in the mix too. According to Professor Ron's website, anxiety and depression often went together in what was termed a 'co-morbid' relationship. It made sense to me. Ever since the long dark London winter when I turned fifteen, I had had to drag myself out of regular lengthy bouts of profound gloom. I'd never sought medication for it, but I understood why others whose gloom was even more crepuscular might need help finding the daylight. Sometimes drugs were the only good solution, at least in the short term. In retrospect, maybe if I had opted for drugs rather than trying to will my anxieties away, my guts wouldn't have paid such a high price.

And why hadn't I? A determination not to allow myself to be 'weak'? All along I'd been convinced that if I just tried hard enough, I could beat this shyness thing. As the daughter of a behavioural scientist, perhaps I had unconsciously absorbed the message that cognitive behaviour therapy—even if self-administered—was a better way to treat psychological distress than popping a pill.

I admired Christopher Lane's painstaking critique of the complex and compromised process by which the DSM II (*Diagnostic and Statistical Manual of Mental Disorders*) had been updated to include the psychiatric labels for social anxiety disorders. It seemed to me, though, that Lane sometimes conflated shyness, introspection and introversion, and that he underestimated the distress that social anxiety could cause for shy, but nonetheless sociable, people.

'Almost overnight,' he wrote, 'shyness and many other routine moods and ailments became bona fide diseases.' Shyness—a 'routine mood'? Not for the people in Professor Ron's video on social phobia—handsome Jon and loud Lisa and sad Eric—with their palpable grief for the years they had wasted being afraid of other humans.

Again I went back to my memories of that birthday party when my legal drug of choice, alcohol, had been off the menu. Tom hadn't been on the wagon that night. He had started drinking even before he arrived. He had seemed perfectly relaxed, at least for the few brief moments when I'd seen him there. Tom was shy, so he said, and although he was rarely drunk, he loved a drink or three as much as I did.

The first time I had invited him to a party with my friends Tom was still using heroin. He arrived at my place sleepy-eyed and slurring. I remember him leaning against the kitchen bench, staring at me with a wonky grin, while all around him my friends drank a bit more quickly and adjusted themselves to the disturbing presence of his fame.

Now I was curious. Had heroin been *his* drug of choice to combat these stupid fears? Tom was away again but I sent him some questions in an email. What effect had heroin had on his shyness?

'My shyness disappeared,' he wrote back. 'Heroin immediately lessened all my anxiety, and the right amount—not too much—made me perfectly at ease.'

Falling in love had done the same for me. It hadn't entirely taken away my physical self-consciousness. That had morphed into a constant state of hyper-awareness of where my body was in relation to Tom's body. But the elation of finding someone whose very presence in the world seemed to be an extension of my own had often made my shyness evaporate, especially in the early days.

So what was Tom's strategy now, I wondered. How did he put himself at ease since he had given up heroin? It was a conversation to be had in person, not on email, so I left it for later. He would be home soon. Hopefully then we would have some time together, at last.

Invisible Him

A friend of mine told me about a middle-aged man she knew who was very shy. *'Painfully* shy,' she said. The shy man had won many awards during a long career as a photographer, often putting himself in physical danger to capture just the right image. A courageous man, she said. If you met him at a party, though, he could scarcely meet your eye. Conversations were almost impossible.

The man behind the camera, not in front of it.

The observer, not the observed.

The capturer, not the captive.

The fearless human with a terrible fear of other humans.

The invisible man.

I wanted to meet him.

My friend sent him a message, asking if he would speak with me. It took a few weeks, but eventually the shy man responded to me by email. He didn't really want to meet up, he wrote, but if I sent him a postal address he was willing to send me a file of newspaper clippings he thought might interest me. Another few weeks later a fat orange envelope arrived in the mail. Inside was a hand-written note:

> Dear Sian,
>
> Please excuse the delay. Other events overtook me. For the last 40 years I have cut out huge numbers of articles about all sorts of things from papers, magazines etc and I was in the midst of a big sort out when you contacted me.
>
> Enclosed are all the articles I have cut out about shyness. When I say all, there are only about ten, which is most surprising. I would have cut out every article I saw on this subject and am therefore amazed there are so few articles about it.
>
> I hope these are useful.
>
> Please return them if possible.
>
> Kind regards,
>
> L

As the yellowing pieces of paper slid out of the envelope, a familiar smell escaped with them, the acrid smell of old printing ink. The smell of my grandfather Stan Prior. 'Pass me a hilary-n-raymond, would you?' I said out loud to no one as I unfolded the first clipping.

> **You Won't Be Snubbed: The story of a man who overcame his fear of approaching strangers.**
> *By Henry Morton Robinson.*
> *The Reader's Digest, August 1964.*

Published in the same month of the same year I was born. My parents were *Reader's Digest* subscribers. I imagined my shy father reading this article when the crying of his newborn daughter woke him in the middle of the night.

Henry Morton Robinson describes meeting a man called David who is willing to talk to anyone, anywhere, with the greatest of ease, melting 'the icy cellophane that most human beings come wrapped in'. Henry confides to his new friend David that all his life he's 'wanted to mingle with strangers who could widen my interests, yet I've always hung back, afraid of a rebuff. How does one overcome this fear of being snubbed?' David delivers a little homily. 'My own fear completely disappears when I remember that the dearest friends I have were once strangers.'

I remembered meeting my friend Gabby, a six-foot-tall stranger who shook my hand firmly in the cramped arts office of the Trades Hall. Gabby took on belligerent abattoir bosses by day and sang sweetly with the altos in the trade union choir by night. She courted my friendship in the pub after rehearsals and I didn't shrink from her overtures because I wasn't Shy Sian in this company. I was Comrade Choir Mistress. The one in charge. I wasn't afraid. In reward for her friendship I gave her solo parts. Blatant favouritism.

The next file to slide out of the photographer's envelope included three pages of ads for a course in 'Auto-Psychology'. The pages weren't dated. From the look of the bouffant hairstyles in the accompanying images, though, they were printed in the mid-sixties too. The course came from somewhere called 'The Institute'. It could be sent to you in instalments in plain sealed envelopes. 'Every care is taken to meet the wishes of Correspondents with regard to privacy.'

Just like porn, I thought. For the purposes of Auto-Pleasuring. Same shame-filled impulse to hide your desires from the world. Except in this instance all you desire is freedom from self-consciousness.

166

The first page announced in bold caps:

HOW TO STOP BEING SHY!

> If you are nervous and shy; if you blush and stammer
> when embarrassed in company, especially in the presence
> of the opposite sex; if you are letting opportunities slip
> through by being too nervous...here is your chance to
> become forceful and red-blooded.

Dear Institute people, I wanted to write back, our blood is
already red. Everyone can see that when we blush. And when
we are angry. Anger makes me brave; red-blooded; forceful.
Not shy at all.

The next page was a series of Questions and their Answers.

> **Q. Is the Course likely to make one Introspective?**
>
> A. On the contrary, the Course does exactly the opposite,
> because it shows you how to 'get outside yourself'. It
> definitely discourages morbid self-examination and
> stimulates creative expression and active co-operation
> with your environment.

I was confused. Surely 'getting outside myself' had been the
problem, not the solution. Standing outside, looking at myself,
then looking at others who were looking at me. Trying to
pre-empt or control what they saw. Rather than just being me.
Inside me. Looking out.

And there was that awful word *morbid*. 'Morbid self-
examination'—is that what I'd been doing with all this shyness
research, all this self-disclosure? What was the point of it all?
To stimulate creative expression?

Page Three: WHAT IS AN INFERIORITY COMPLEX?

An Inferiority Complex is a disturbance in the Subconscious Mind which manifests itself in Self-Consciousness and Lack of Confidence—in nervousness and 'nerviness'—in causeless worry—in depression and sense of futility—in lassitude and lack of enterprise—in weakness of will and habits... These are symptoms of 'something wrong' within your personality which you can put right—the effect of conflicting forces within yourself or the result of some emotional experience or some destructive influence during your personality development.

Those capitals were so authoritative. So irrefutable. Lack of Confidence. Inferiority Complex. Did I believe I was inferior to other people? It was a question I had put to Professor Ron in our interview.

PROFESSOR RON: If you're asking me do shy people perceive others as better than they are, then the answer is no. People with social anxiety are pretty accurate at assessing others' performance and attractiveness and abilities. They're just not very accurate with their own. But they don't dislike themselves normally. That's linked more with depression, and social phobia and depression often go together. But they're not the same thing. There are a lot of social-phobic people who are not depressed at all and don't have that self-dislike.

As for the 'emotional experience' that triggered this 'causeless worry', perhaps the Institute People who sent out those furtive parcels of assertiveness in the mail hadn't yet heard about temperament theory and how we were all born somewhere on the approach–withdrawal spectrum. That's what Professor Margot had told me.

There had been that one time, though, during our shyness interview beside the walnut piano when she had stepped outside the boundaries of temperament theory. When Margot had wondered aloud about the weeks that followed Glen's death. Those long days and longer nights when the fear must have gripped her so tight she could hardly breathe. When she might in turn have held on tight to that newborn child during the long months after the brave shy father stepped back into the waves and disappeared. Just that once she had wondered aloud about whether fear might have passed through her rigid body and into mine, a bitter cocktail of breastmilk and liquid terror.

At the bottom of the cinematographer's pile of clippings was a newspaper article from some time in the 1980s. Prince Charles and Princess Diana smiled awkwardly at the camera, her long vulnerable neck tilted at that shy angle. 'HOW TO BEAT SHYNESS...' the headline read. Both members of the royal couple are shy, the author told us.

'Shy people are besieged with negative thoughts...Fear of rejection is behind all shyness. It is important that a shy person makes him or herself do, every day, an action that they fear.' Exposure therapy, they call that.

But when is taking action that you fear a good thing, and when is it foolish? Did my anxious father fear going into the surf that day? Or was all fear banished the moment he decided to try and help?

On Mortality

Sometimes when I'm at a surf beach I half expect to see him out there, floating serenely in the waves. He's enjoying the feel of the water on his broad shoulders, the warmth of the sun on his wet scalp. He'll come in soon and towel off, squinting into the glare, and then he'll smile at me with my own shy smile, my mirror-face. We'll sit together under a striped umbrella and watch the families gathered in little clutches around their blue and white Eskies or spread out in human join-the-dots patterns, playing with wet tennis balls. The children with sand clinging to their legs, women tugging at their bikinis, men standing in pairs at the water's edge, arms crossed in identical poses as they exchange information about the latest cricket scores.

But that's not how the beach looked that day. That day the beach was wind-whipped, empty, until the busload of blinking orchestral musicians piled out onto the sand. A day when no one should have been swimming but some couldn't resist. That's what I've been told. I think. I can't be sure now.

There were two of them leading the way to the water's edge,

young ones, feeling immortal. I picture them hopping over the waves, their pale musicians' arms flapping at the froth under the scudding clouds. Then quickly sucked out beyond the shallows by the furtive rip. Arms flapping harder now, salt water leaping into their mouths. Frog-legs kicking. Frog-voices croaking uselessly under the roar of the breakers.

And the father suddenly forgetting about himself and hauling off his shirt. Running now, away from his wife and children and into the clutching water. Those trumpeter's lungs breathing deep, that blond head diving over and under the waves as he heads for the furthest immortal.

The rest of the orchestra watching, not breathing, as the slow-motion father reaches the furthest immortal and puts his hand under a chin and hauls the young body backwards through the overtaking waves until he can feel the sand under his feet.

Is this what happened? Or was there a rope around his waist and a silent group of onlookers at the other end, slow-motion-tugging them back to shore? I'm not sure. I have to fill in the gaps for you. And for me.

The rest of the orchestra is watching, breathing again, as the first immortal staggers onto the shore. But the father turns (isn't one enough? why so helpful?) and goes out again. He's tiring now, trumpeter's lungs seared with salt, legs kicking slower, but he makes it to the gulping violinist. Again that strong hand under a chin, and the slow progress away from the horizon. The onlookers turn to each other, shaking their heads in amazement. A hero!

My mother looks down at her eldest daughter and mouths 'yes' in response to a question that can hardly be heard over the whipping wind.

And when they all turn back the second immortal is safe.

Safe but alone.

The father has disappeared.

I imagine it as an upside-down pyramid of suffering in the remnants of our family that day, gradually diluting as it goes down the family structure. Margot first: pure scarifying misery. But how can I conjure that?

My five-year-old sister is next, the one who had asked our mother, 'Is he coming back?' The one to whom Margot replied, 'Yes.' (But did my sister really say that? Have I made it up? Embellished the story?)

Then my brother, nearly two years old and so like his father already, everybody says so, the spitting image. Holding on to our mother's legs for dear life as the sand whips around his chubby ankles.

And at the bottom of the pyramid there is me, the three-month-old baby, blissfully unaware. Safe in Margot's arms, eyes shielded from the whipping sand by a soft blanket. But I feel her heartbeat. It thuds against my ear, too fast. I feel her chest rising and falling as the fear sucks the air from her oboist's lungs. I feel her arms tightening around me.

Perhaps too tight.

There is a photo I've seen (or do I imagine I've seen?) in another yellowing news clipping. Pinned up at my grandfather Stan Prior's place, maybe. A woman is standing on a beach. Standing where the wet sand meets the dry, looking out to sea. She looks so alone, in spite of the three small children with her. She's waiting, as I sometimes do, to see those shoulders rise above the waves and begin the slow swim back to shore.

172

Perhaps it's not a photo I remember but a dream. I wonder if all four of us have had variations on the same one. He waits until we're asleep and then he appears way out beyond the breakers and he's swimming towards us. Pretty soon he's stumbling through the shallows to the shore, tired but safe. We're relieved but we're also angry. Where have you been all these years? we ask. Why didn't you come back? Didn't you realise we'd be worried sick? Did you think about us at all before you leapt into the surf to save someone else's children?

Sometimes when I'm swimming in surf I dive under the waves and stay down there while the water pummels my legs. I try to imagine how it must have felt for him in those last moments. Did he crash into some hidden rocks and then know nothing more? Or did he feel that pummelling too and fight to be able to breathe again? I wait until my lungs are screaming and then I surface, gasping like a fish, and stumble through the shallows to the shore, tired but safe. Like my dream father.

So Temperamental

The beeping started before dawn. My dreams mutated from the usual mass drownings to smoke alarms going off in buildings where the flames are licking the walls and people are trapped. Alarum alarum. Beep beep. Half waking, I remembered it was the tip-truck arriving to carry the topsoil away from The Somme (as Tom and I had christened the muddy building site next door to our home).

I found a pair of pre-loved earplugs under my pillow and jammed them in. Even then the noise was barely muffled. Beep beep. My teeth grinding was getting worse.

The beeping continued all day. In between beeps, there were revs and rumbles, shouts and whistles, and the occasional seismic judder when the earth needed more punishment from a bigger machine. The constant noise made me feel as if I'd grown a pair of miniature jackhammers just below my earlobes. The empty paddock next door was about to be colonised by a five-storey apartment building. Tom and I had briefly considered selling up and moving out. But who would want this place now? Tom suggested it might be worth approaching a government department to see if they'd be interested in buying the house for its heritage value, because of his status as a famous Australian songwriter, but I was dubious.

If only we could leave town. Ever since Tom had returned from his latest trip I had been fantasising about weekends in the country. Nights in chilly B and Bs with frilly bedspreads. The way the silence pressed down on my eardrums like a masseur easing a knot of muscle. Lying awake listening to the absence of sound. The blissful quiet.

I was teaching in a writing course and it was time for marking. The assignment on the top of the pile was from a woman who was writing a book about babies and parenting. Her extract was entitled *Temperament*. Sheesh. Even when I wasn't actively researching this stuff, it was following me around.

> Shyness-Hypersensitivity: Some children seem to be fearful of anything new in their lives—people, food, places, and even new toys. With stimuli such as noise or light, those children's reactions will occur at a low level. If a noise is annoying, some children will react with a very strong response (crying, yelling, covering ears, jumping around, whinging) while other children will simply find a way to avoid the noise. Some children are viscerally hypersensitive all the time and have no way of understanding why they cannot bear the stimulus.

I remembered being about eleven years old. The noise from Yoni's bedroom was driving me crazy. She was sixteen and in a year's time she'd be gone, off in search of new people, food, places, embracing life with an abandon that filled me with horror—and envy. But right now she was listening to the new Pink Floyd album on her little blue record player, and so we all were.

The guitar riff snaked out from under her door and slithered down the hallway to the room I shared with my brother. I was lying on my bed, teeth gritted, trying to read. It was impossible. Stomping down the hall, I found my mother working in the soundproof study that doubled as our music practice room.

'Mum, Yoni won't turn the music DOWN,' I protested. 'It's not FAIR. I can't CONCENTRATE. Mum? Can you TELL her?' My teary voice rose and fell like an ambulance siren.

Decades later my sister the actor could still mimic, to the precise semi-tone, the pitch of my whining. 'Mum', she would carol, 'Yoni won't let me put my CLOTHES on, Mum! Yoni is sitting on my CLOTHES and she won't let me put them ON.'

I had to laugh, every time, because she was funny. But I could still feel that child's anger, her skin-crawling, teeth-gritting irritation with loud noises, bright lights, big crowds, strong flavours, cold weather, a whiff of acrid perfume, sand stuck between her toes or a scratchy woollen jumper rubbing at her neck.

There had been a primary school camp. Endless hot walks through coastal heath and, at the end of one hike, a Special Treat. A giant mud-pool that we were allowed, no, *encouraged* to jump into, fully clothed. I remembered the squealing, near-hysterical joy of my schoolmates, used to being herded by parents away from all mud-puddles, now being given carte blanche to *wallow*, and my own silent near-panic at the thought of getting dirty, of having to walk all the way back to camp caked with crusty black mud, of all the washing involved. Worse, almost, than being asked to strip naked. And I remembered the strange shame of my goody-goody cleanliness when we finally turned back towards camp.

As I read my student's neat summary of my own temperament traits, I found myself wondering if hypersensitivity made everyday living kind of...painful. There was a layer of skin missing, a protective membrane, or so it seemed.

And what did my mother make of this difficult child and her complaints? An anxious child with a tendency to sulk when life's settings weren't quite perfect. A child with an insatiable appetite for affection. A watchful child. A vigilant analyst of fairness and favouritism. A nurser and rehearser of grievances. A weeper, a fretter, a clinger, a grizzler. A child for whom a slumber party was an endurance marathon in separation anxiety. Was Margot sick to death of it all? Or did my mother's growing understanding of temperament psychology allow her to stand back and get the measure of her youngest child, perched precariously up one end of the Shyness-Hypersensitivity seesaw?

The hypersensitivity had never gone away. This princess still felt the peas. Even without the Battle of the Somme going on next door, I needed earplugs to get to sleep most nights. But my student had given me another piece of the jigsaw puzzle: 'It can be argued,' she wrote, 'that it is perhaps shyness in combination with high reactivity which contributes to vulnerability for anxiety problems, rather than shyness alone.'

Maybe I wasn't just a shy person. Maybe I was a viscerally hypersensitive over-reactive socially anxious shy person. How exhausting—for me and for everyone around me.

Self / Other

At last Tom and I were going away together for a weekend. It was my birthday and I wanted to celebrate with him. He had been travelling off and on for three months out of the last nine and missing him had been like nursing a permanent bruise. Besides, off and on had never suited me. To avoid those flickers of stranger-danger, even in my closest relationships, I needed frequent close contact, a regular groove. Thanks to one of my university lecturers, I thought I understood why.

Political scientist Dr Graham Little had introduced me to a theory he had developed about social relationships, which was that we all favoured one of three styles of relating to others—one of three distinct friendship modes.

The first friendship mode he called 'Self-vs-Other'. These were the people whose social relationships were essentially competitive and utilitarian. They were the strategists, looking for order and opportunity in friendship. 'If you scratch my back I'll scratch yours, and just quietly, I'll prove I'm a better back scratcher than you.'

The second mode was called 'Self-in-Other'. These were the people who sought a sense of solidarity and community with others. They avoided competition if they could and instead looked for security and social connection in relationships. They were the co-operators, the empathisers, the communicators. 'Solidarity Forever' could well have been their theme song.

· The final mode was called 'Self-and-Other'. These were the people who were much more interested in inspiring or being inspired by their friends rather than in being helped, or helpful to, them. They were the confident, charismatic ones, the leaders whose authority came from their ability to generate new, interesting and even risky ideas.

My anxious brain was attracted to this neat little list. I was also sceptical about whether something as complex as friendship could be reduced to something so simplistic. The list stuck with me, though, and over the years I sometimes used it to try to work out whether I should feel safe with certain people.

I had never seen myself as belonging to the first mob, the Self-vs-Other utilitarians. When it came to engaging with other humans, back-scratching had never been my forte, nor strategising. I had always been too awkward, or too direct. Too awkwardly direct. Or perhaps shyness had rendered me so socially underskilled that I couldn't even *try* to turn a relationship to my advantage. I didn't like these people very much, didn't trust them, didn't want to have to compete with them. Besides, they were the ones who were usually most adept at small talk and I had never been good at that stuff.

Occasionally, though, I envied them. I watched them manoeuvring in the workplace, manoeuvring at the pub, manoeuvring others into place around them. Watched them figuring out how other people could help them to get what they wanted. I envied their breezy extroversion, their smooth-talking ways, their career-ladder-climbing success. I envied the way they rarely wasted emotional energy on dumb things like fear of negative evaluation. They just got on with the business of life.

Self-in-Other, though, they were more my kind of people. I met a lot of them in the environment movement and the trade union choir. Helpful people. People who believed that working alongside other people, rather than competing with them, was the best way to get things done. They were loyal friends, the ones who wanted to see you regularly and not because they wanted anything from you. They just wanted to stay in touch, to keep up with the soap opera of your emotional life. My grandmother Peg was part of the Self-in-Other gang. Nothing gave her more pleasure than putting herself at the service of others. In a previous decade I had lived for nine years with a man who fitted this profile perfectly. Self-in-Other people made you feel safe.

The ones I was most drawn to, though, were the third mob: Self-and-Other. I could list them: Sally, Marie, Mieke, even Tom, in spite of his quiet ways. The charismatic ones who drew others towards them with an invisible force, like the magnets in Stan Prior's printing shed. They were the ones I always hoped would notice me because I rarely found the courage to approach them. Too shy to make the first move. Too busy with what the psychologists would call my 'safety behaviours': avoiding eye contact; staying on the edge of groups; rehearsing an escape plan. I was an expert at all of those. Perhaps you could add to that list maintaining monogamous sexual relationships.

'Vigilant and anxious reactivity to stressful or challenging situations': this had been on the Chinese psychologist's list of shyness-inhibition symptoms. What could be more stressful or vigilance-inducing than constantly wondering who else your beloved might be loving? Whose deliciously novel amorous repertoire might lead them to negatively evaluate your own wearyingly familiar one? I couldn't bear it.

When Tom and I first got together, the question of fidelity *v.* promiscuity had been one of the biggest knots for us to untangle. Nothing else caused us as much grief, except perhaps his heroin use.

I could find ways to cope with his frequent long absences. He always wrote to me while he was travelling and I wrote back, every day. Hundreds of thousands of precious words, each one a crumb on the trail that would eventually lead him back to me.

I could find a way to cope with the editors who rejected my proffered articles but would virtually go down on bended knee to ask Tom for some of his prose writing. I couldn't promise not to grumble about it, but I would cope. There was a perverse pleasure in knowing that occasionally he used some of my writing, sometimes entire paragraphs from my columns (with permission), in the material he would offer to those grateful editors.

I could find a way to cope when I became invisible in his company, when the new people we met together became focused on keeping his attention and forgot to include me in the conversation. I understood the deep pleasure of winning his attention.

I could find a way to cope with the daily email inquiries from correspondents wanting me to forward their requests directly to Tom so they didn't have to run the gauntlet of his manager. I knew I wasn't his personal assistant, even if they didn't.

I could find a way to cope with his multitudinous fans and their autograph-hunting, photograph-taking presence in our lives. Even the obsessed ones who sent me emails describing me as

'Beyond Disgusting' and a 'Bitch Prostitute' and threatening me with a 'Bloodbath' for my 'Mountain of Faults'. I deleted their emails and told myself I was glad not to be living in their skin.

And I could even find a way to cope (just) when he took the morsels of grief I shared with him in the dark and turned them into songs.

But unless Tom gave up using heroin and fucking other women, I couldn't feel safe. The choice was his: them or me.

He had been reluctant. By all accounts a needle full of heroin feels pretty good. I had never wanted to find out for myself. As for fucking other women—it wasn't a moral thing. I understood the pleasures of wanting and being wanted.

There had been that one time for me, towards the end of an earlier relationship, the one-off indiscretion that becomes the beginning of the end. Forbidden pleasures often turn out to be so much less pleasurable than you anticipate. Once you've broken the rules and got away with it, though, it can be hard to find a reason not to break them again. 'Don't pull on a thread,' my grandmother Peg used to tell me. 'The whole thing could come apart.' And it had. That's when I realised I had to be monogamous. To stop things unravelling.

Of course I understood that charismatic Self-and-Other people usually get a lot of offers and that *famous* charismatic Self-and-Other people like Tom probably get more offers than they can poke a stick at. But it wasn't something I could live with. I offered to walk away, no hard feelings, if Tom preferred those pleasures to being with me.

Eventually Tom had agreed, on both counts. Heroin had been killing too many of his friends lately. As for monogamy, he consoled himself out loud with the quote attributed to the actor Paul Newman: 'Why go out for hamburgers when you've got steak at home?' I winced at the raw-meat comparison, but it was at least some kind of 'positive evaluation'.

But after all our time apart in recent months, the old itch of anxiety had resurfaced. It had to be scratched. Over my birthday dinner at a country hotel I posed the question: 'Monogamy's not so bad after all, is it?'

It was a rhetorical question. We were the lucky ones, the ones who had found each other. Found ourselves-in-another. Tom looked away for a moment then smiled and took my hand across the table. 'You needn't worry,' he said. 'I am true to you. You make monogamy a good place to be.'

Still safe then.

Don't Look

Back in town, an email request arrived. A team of film producers was making a feature-length documentary about Tom, and his family and friends were all going to be involved. Was I willing to be interviewed?

I was torn. There was plenty to say and I wanted to be able to help. But the thought of sitting in front of a camera, trying to sound lucid and insightful while answering questions about someone I loved, filled me with anxiety (of course). I asked Tom what he thought, half hoping he would tell me not to worry, that there were plenty of others with plenty to say. He told me that he'd retained final editorial control over the film. That meant he must have had a view on who should be interviewed, but he gave nothing away. So I said yes. And for the next few nights I lay awake at 3 a.m., heart racing, trying not to think about posterity.

Or that camera.

When I was working in radio in the 1990s, television came sniffing around me every couple of years like a curious dog.

Someone had heard me on air or seen me at an ABC event. Someone had said something to somebody about me. There would be a call from someone with an overly familiar phone manner inviting me to do a screen test. Somebody somewhere was making a pilot for some new arts program or current affairs show or talking-heads panel. Someone thought I might be suitable for the job, and wanted me to come to a studio for a try-out. Television has always been a medium with an insatiable appetite for new faces.

Each time that call came through I would have two simultaneous and opposite reactions. I would be flattered by the attention and excited about the possibility of Having A Say on national television (television! where everyone's hair stays in place and everyone speaks in perfectly grammatical sentences and no one is in two minds about anything). And I would be terrified by the thought of looking into that camera.

But which of those two made me say yes every time—the flattery or the terror?

Here's what I remember:

It's 1998 and I'm sitting on a sagging purple couch, trying to look relaxed and comfortable. I don't know what to do with my hands. Surrounding me on the couch is a flotilla of leopard-print cushions. A woman with skintight jeans has just finished pointing a sawn-off blow dryer at my head. My lips have been painted into a glistening pout. Mascara-laden lashes frame my vision like torn fly-wire. And beside me on the couch lounges a rock star in a brown shirt. I haven't heard of him before and it's going to be a problem.

I'm here to audition for the pilot of a funky new pop culture show and they want me to interview funky Mr Brown Shirt. The producers have given me no warning about who the 'talent' is, and no chance to prepare. They just want us to have a chat. The rock star is wearing a brown shirt unbuttoned to just above his diaphragm. Maybe he wants me to talk to his chest hair. Or to his three-day growth. I don't want to talk to him at all. What am I doing here? But the camera is waiting.

Leaning back a fraction (that brown shirt hasn't been washed since the last gig, I'd bet a month's rent on it) I swivel my stiff neck towards the camera until I'm looking directly into that circle of blackness. I try to imagine it's a person. That's what I've been advised.

Imagine it's your closest friend.

Imagine it's your grandmother.

Imagine it's someone who loves you.

Imagine it's someone who needs your help.

(My imagination is failing me.)

Imagine it's a reflective window hiding a team of miniature psychologists: *Anxious, hmmm, very anxious.*

The camera's looking at me and now I'm looking at him but he's looking at the woman in the skinny jeans who's hovering in the background with her hairdryer at the ready, just in case. He's giving her a special smile. I'm trying to think of some funky small talk to start the conversation but all I can think about is the camera looking at me.

I'm used to being prepared. I'm used to making sure I don't need to improvise, doing the research, preparing an angle, having a list of questions ready. Ensuring I have a fallback position. But that's not what they want from me here. They want me to Have A Chat.

But I don't do chat, I want to tell the camera. *I do interviews. Conversations with a beginning, a middle and an end. Orderly interactions that I can control. Interactions for the efficient delivery of information, not verbal playtime with a rock star, the exact nature of whose oeuvre currently escapes me.*

I have a stab. I ask about his latest album. About his recent gigs. Whether he has any touring plans. But nothing flows. There are awkward pauses. Between his answers. And my questions. He seems faintly bored. Eventually he gives up looking at me and begins speaking directly to the camera, giving that black circle his best rock star smile, as if it's his best friend's new girlfriend.

I am a ventriloquist, pleading silently with the camera. *He should be fronting this funky TV show, not me.* The camera stares malevolently back at me. Mute.

I never did get a gig on television.

So disappointed.

So relieved.

Mostly relieved.

I didn't want to work in that stoopid shallow medium anyway, I told myself each time. I had no real investment in that screen test. I wasn't interested in learning how to speak Televisionese. Radio was the medium for people like me (invisible people). The camera wasn't rejecting me. *I* was rejecting the camera, I told myself.

In our family photo albums my sister Yoni is always looking directly into the lens. Sitting in dappled sunlight with baby Sian on her lap, she looks like a Madonna-in-training. In a group shot with all our blonde Prior cousins, she is grinning as if she's just been made the boss of us all. In a studio photo at the beginning of her acting career she is the seductress, looking back over her shoulder, daring us to resist her golden beauty. The camera loves her and she knows it.

In those family albums there are dozens of images in which I appear to be striking a pose: the same pose every time. My head is tilted to the left, chin pointing towards my right shoulder, left shoulder slightly raised. Eyes squinting, smile tight. On the front porch in a pink tutu, feet splayed, aged six. In front of a music stand, holding a clarinet, aged ten. Leaning on a balcony, new green frock, sixteenth birthday. Sitting on a couch, wine glass in hand, twenty-first birthday. The head tilted, always tilted, as if it's trying to escape from the torso. Leave the rest of the body to deal with the camera's gaze.

Please don't look at me.

And yet, Prior. There is the matter of the short-lived modelling career. How do you explain that? Flattered—again. *Look at me.* Shy, but a show-off.

Here's what I remember:

It's 1982 and I'm standing on a suburban beach, trying to decide between another swim and another ice-cream. My final school exams finished two weeks ago and most days it feels like I deserve at least three ice-creams. I notice a blonde woman in her late thirties staring at me from her lounge chair. She notices me noticing her, rises more gracefully than anyone should ever be allowed to rise from a lounge chair, and comes over. 'Are you a model?' she asks.

Are you *kidding*? I blush and shake my head.

'I run a modelling agency and I wondered if you'd like to come and talk to me about joining. I think you have the look of today.'

The look of today: a collection of words that belong on a screwed-up piece of paper at the bottom of a rubbish bin in a windowless room in the basement of a third-rate advertising agency.

Deep inside my head, though, there lurks a homunculus of the Austr-alien schoolgirl in London with her chunky jeans and her dodgy haircut, her lonely lunch hours and her ambiguous gender. She's sick of hiding in the library. She's decided she wants to be a Woman. In fact, she wants to be the kind of Woman that other women want to be. The kind of Woman that men want. She wants to be Magazine Woman.

So I take the business card that is offered to me and on the way home I make sure it doesn't get wet inside my beach bag. It takes me a few weeks but eventually I find the courage to call the number on the business card and the process begins.

The blonde woman is called Fiona and she used to be a model herself. Her facial features are so even, I find myself staring covertly at them in our meetings, looking for a flaw. This is in the days before Botox injections and facial reconstructions had become as common as leg waxing. That perfectly symmetrical face of hers is probably the real deal. As she sits on the other side of an empty desk in her light-filled office by the bay, inducting me into the strange rituals of the modelling world, I am often distracted by my search for those non-existent flaws.

First there are The Shots. Fiona sends me to the suburban home of her photographer friend, another absurdly even-featured woman in her thirties, whose living room is lit up like a small football stadium. She instructs me to remove my chunky spectacles and put on the bathers I'd been wearing at the beach that day. She paints my face until I hardly recognise myself in the mirror. She puts handfuls of gel in my hair ('The Wet Look is in'), draws lines around my lips so they look cartoon-sized ('The Full-Lipped Look is in'), tells me to lie on my side on her light-drenched lounge suite and asks me to pout.

As her children argue on the other side of the living room about which TV show they want to watch, the photographer leans in close, pointing the camera at me. My face aches from pouting. The camera clicks and clicks. Because my hand is on the side of my head, preventing it from tilting away from the black clicking circle, my chin draws further and further into my neck.

I am not a model.

I am a slow-blinking tortoise on a lounge suite.

I am an amphibian in a one-piece bathing suit.

I am a web-footed creature stranded on a sun-bleached rock.

I am trying to pretend that I am invisible.

Look at me.

Please don't look at me.

At last it is over.

But because a part of my brain has already decided that whatever frightens me most, that is the thing I must do, it's not really over.

Fiona the modelling agent puts in a bulk order for something called a composite card. This is a glossy black and white calling card on which are printed several light-drenched photos of the pouting tortoise, its first name and its vital statistics. When the cards are ready I am sent on a series of go-sees.

This involves ringing up a list of advertising agencies, photographic houses and fashion magazines and telling them that I'm new to the agency. Would they like to look me over? If they say yes, I put on the pouting mask of make-up and go-see them.

'Had much experience?' Fiona has strongly advised me to lie. She has even suggested some lines.

'Oh-yes-I've-just-come-down-from-Sydney-where-I-was-doing-some-work-for-Fosseys.' What even IS Fosseys?

'How are your legs?' That one throws me. I nearly say, 'Fine thanks, how are yours?'

Waiting for job interviews is possibly the worst part. Lining up on comfy chairs outside the casting person's office with ten other girls, all of whom presumably also have The Look of Today. Girls with full lips and no hips. Girls with aggressive smiles and submissive hairdos. So many sets of flawless features in such a small space. So little apparent self-consciousness. What strange planet is this?

I never land a modelling job if there has been a screen test involved. Sometimes I see a fashion ad on TV and recognise it as one I've gone for. Watching those slim young things giggling and wriggling their way across the screen, I silently thank the camera for its judgment, for sparing me this indignity. Still, though, I don't give up.

Once every few months someone offers me a job simply on the basis of the photos on the composite card. A costume hire company dresses me in a nineteenth-century ladies riding outfit, complete with tall hat and riding crop. They send a black limo to drive me to every advertising agency in the city, where I hand-deliver invitations to their annual costume ball. Clambering out of that four-wheeled coffin onto busy city pavements, trying not to lose my hat, I feel like a reanimated corpse condemned to wander among the staring pedestrians of the late twentieth century. Partially reanimated. There is always that stiffness, the creeping rigor of the physically self-conscious.

It didn't end with a bang. Not even with a whimper. I just stopped calling Fiona at the agency. Eventually she stopped calling me too. The pile of composite cards was consigned to the bottom drawer of my desk, which was covered in university library books about feminism. I was learning about The Patriarchy and The Male Gaze and how together they produce strange ideas like The Look of Today, an idea that makes girls with less than perfectly even features feel deeply imperfect. (The limo driver copped a lecture from me about The Evils of the Male Gaze. Plenty to say, even back then, when I found a cause more powerful than my own fears.) If I'm honest, though, it was technology as much as ideology that made me give up on modelling in the end. That camera. That all-seeing, all-knowing lens.

I still have a paper bag full of those yellowing composite cards. I know exactly where it is. Down the bottom of a big wooden chest, hidden underneath decades of collected letters from friends and garish family photo albums. If I wanted to, I could dig out those cards and have another look at that pouting girl in her one-piece bathers. The siren of the suburbs. Try to see what the camera saw three decades ago.

I never dig them out and I never show them to anyone.

It is my little brown paper bag of shame.

The team of blokes making the documentary about Tom arrived at our house in a tangle of extension cords and camera equipment. I had put on some make-up and my face felt stiff with foundation. And with fear. Who was it who first described the camera as a 'mirror with a memory'? Perched on the edge of a chair in our dining room, I tried to calm my breathing while the blokes checked the light levels.

The interviewer, a small intense man who sat too close to me, opened with a question about Tom's writing voice. As I began speaking I could feel the fear draining out of my body like a hot bath slowly emptying. Of course. This wasn't about me. This was about something much bigger than me. I was a proselytiser, here to persuade people that Tom was extraordinary. I had cover. Camera? What camera?

I spoke about the rhythm of Tom's writing, about the poetry

hiding beneath the simplicity, about how his words had resonated with me, about witnessing fans trembling in his presence. When the interviewer asked about Tom's heroin habit and whether he gave it up 'for me', I shook my head. The last thing I wanted was to be defined as the Good Influence here. Forever frozen on screen in helpful mode. I wouldn't be the shy girl with her gentle moral persuasions, the character who had escaped from the pages of *Little Women*. Not for posterity. No way.

'It was his choice,' I said. 'I told him what I thought about it and then I left it up to him.'

The interviewer wasn't happy with my response. A salvation story required an angel and I wasn't playing my part. He asked the same question in a slightly different way. My journalist's brain admired his persistence. I would have done the same. 'It was his choice, his decision,' I said, smiling beatifically into the camera's shining lens.

Then This

An ordinary day. Minding Tom's three-year-old grandson together, a child for whom I would fight off a pride of hungry lions.

Tom kicked a football to him. I let him have a little go at holding on to the buzzing electric mower with me while I tidied up our life.

A trip to the theatre. I wore a grey striped dress.

'You look like a symphony in silver,' Tom said as we left the house.

Pos re. I was warm all over.

The play was *Hamlet*. An interactive version. Which way would the Danish prince jump? It was up to the audience members to decide. (I was defensive on Shakespeare's behalf. Call me old-fashioned, but why mess with the original story?)

The madness was convincing, nevertheless.

When Ophelia said, 'We know what we are, but know not what we may be,' I thought about what else I may be if I could stop being shy. Or stop worrying about being shy.

At interval a photographer from the Sunday paper asked Tom for a photo.

Tom grabbed me by the waist and smiled into the camera's lens. Click click.

On the way home Tom's phone beeped repeatedly. While I drove he was busy reading his text messages.

'I have to do a photo shoot. At six. In the morning,' he said.

So early? Those cameras again.

We'd been together for ten years.

We were home by eleven.

Into the bedroom.

Then this.

We need to talk, he said. *I've decided I want to be single again.*

A shock of scalding heat flushed through my ribcage.

The air was sucked out of my lungs and then my heart began its race to outrun those words. Suddenly I was not standing but sitting. On the bed we had shared for a decade.

Oh, I said to the red rug on the polished floorboards. *Wow. This is big*, I told my knees as all the flesh above and below them turned to liquid. Stupid, small words.

My hands clutched at the blue bedspread, trying to steady my torso against the shuddering force of that heartbeat.

When I spoke again there was so little air in my lungs my words were just above a whisper. It was someone else's voice speaking these words.

Why?

I want to be able to be with other women. I don't want to be in a long-term relationship with just one person.

Oh.   But.   Is there someone else?

No. There's no one else.

IS there someone else?

No.

It didn't make sense.

Have there been others?

Yes. I have been with other women. But there's no one in particular. I don't want to be in a relationship anymore. I'm sorry.

Finally it had caught me.

All those years of tiptoeing around it, of risk-avoiding and safety-net securing, of *what if*-ing and *better not*-ing and rejecting others before I could be rejected, of withdrawing and giving up before I'd even tried, of choosing only those I thought would never leave.

Now this.

The sudden dissolving of all that was once solid.

Nothing but wet grey mud inside me, around me, on top of me.

Fight or flight?

I could not fight this.

I hauled myself up, every particle trembling, and escaped the room. Into the next room, pacing for ten long seconds, what to do, where to go? Out again, back to the red rug room, grabbed my mobile, out again, down the hall, into the lounge room, shaking fingers tapping my sister's number onto the glowing screen. From the edge of the couch I whispered into the phone.

Yoni are you still up? Can I come over?

Back down the hall, into the red rug room. Tom was sitting on the end of the bed, head down. I reached up to grab the black suitcase on top of the wardrobe but it was so high, too high, and my treacherous fingers couldn't reach. I stretched and failed and failed again. Pathetic.

Tom left. Went to another room, I don't know where. The other end of the house. As far away from my stretching, shaking hands as possible. I found a chair and placed it in front of the mirror attached to the wardrobe door, the mirror that had watched us sliding in and out of each other for so many years, watched us liquefying each other in the big blue bed.

Clutching at the suitcase I climbed down from the chair and scuttled around the room like a startled insect. I was grabbing things and shovelling them inside in fast-motion, a cartoon character packing a cartoon suitcase, my clothes spilling out over the sides, my shaking hands struggling with the zips.

And yet, some part of me was very sensible. Very helpful. Ticking things off a mental list.

- Take earplugs, sleep will be hard.
- And an eye-mask.
- Take your thyroid pills, you'll need those.
- And lanolin for dry lips.
- Take hankies, you will need hankies.
- Bathers and goggles, you will need to swim.

What sort of a strange holiday was I packing for here?

A holiday on the island of grief.

I zipped up the suitcase and headed for the door and I was out and almost running to the gate with the suitcase lurching and jerking behind me and now I was at the car and I pressed the blue button and opened the door and threw the suitcase across and fell into the driver's seat.

As

The Boys disappeared down the end of the driveway

The Father walked into the surf

The Lover withdrew his love

and I was alone.

But not safe. Not now. Not yet.

Not for a long time.

Two further definitions of the word shy:
- To move suddenly in fright or alarm.
- To come up short, insufficient, less.

Sunday Paper

On the back page of the Sunday paper the famous songwriter leaned into his beloved, a proprietary hand on her hip. She wore a grey striped dress and stood up straight, except for her head, which was tilted slightly to the left, chin pointing towards her right shoulder. Her left shoulder was slightly raised, her eyes squinting, her smile tight.

Please don't look at me.

Yes, look at me.

Don't believe what you see.

PART TWO

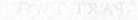

Four Thirty-Three

There is no sleep. There is just my fast-beating heart. It comes with me to my sister's bathroom where there are too many mirrors, too firmly attached. I turn my head away from them as I fill and drink glass after glass of water. At 2:21 a.m. At 4:33. And again at 6:11. Glass after glass, until I am pure liquid. Nothing can quench this thirst. Not enough water, not enough air.

Because I am not enough.

Food is almost impossible. No room, too much liquid, even though most of the liquid seems to be spilling out from the holes between my forehead and my cheekbones. And the lump in my throat is back, after all these years, threatening to block any solids I try to send down there. Is it another ingot of unspoken words, everything I could have said to Tom before he made this decision about my future? Or a swelling of protest against his silence, his subterfuge? Too late.

The day after I flee to my sister's place a short email arrives from Tom, offering to pay for me to live somewhere else for a while. Offering me money so as not to have to be close to me.

But I need to be near people who want to hold me close or I will drown. A few days after that, there is a phone call.

I don't understand, I tell him. *I need you to help me to understand.*

The thought of being with any woman for the rest of my life makes me feel like I'm in a cage.

But I'm not 'any woman'. I'm this woman. The woman you chose. Because you liked who you were when you were with her.

You mean the thought of being with me *makes you feel like you're in a cage?* My voice has dropped half an octave.

I'm sorry but I need more variety. With more women.

Variety? Hadn't I given him variety? Here, let me list them all:
Shy Sian
   Show-Off Sian
      Smart Sian
     Silly Sian
       Sexy Sian
        Sulky Sian
          Sympathetic Sian
         Shameless Sian
        Singing Sian
          Social Butterfly Sian
          Hold the Fort Sian
         Welcome Home Sian
        Take the Photo Sian
         Creative Collaborator Sian
       Opinionated Sian
      Acquiescent Sian
     Grumpy Sian
    Good Influence Sian
     De Facto Stepmother Sian
    De Facto Step-Grandmother Sian.

I contain multitudes. I am a one-woman variety show.

But 'one woman' seems to be the problem here. I can be all of those people but I can only offer Tom one body.

A final question. It is rhetorical.

If I said to you, 'Okay, no worries, have as many women as you like, we can still be together,' what would you say?

There are several long moments of silence. Then I hang up.

Belonging and Apart

I thought it was an ocean, this love. Vast, endless, embracing around the corners of continents. But it was a mere tarn, a small body of water trickling into a smaller body of water and then into another even smaller, constantly emptying until it was all gone.

The days can be got through, just. There is still work: classes to be taught, articles to be written, songs to be learned. Work has worked for me before, as temporary respite from fear. And I don't have a better plan.

I make lists of all the work to be done and whenever the liquefaction threatens to drown me I sit down at the desk in my sister's spare room and work my way through the tedious lists. I feel like an impostor, someone pretending to be Sian until the real Sian can be found. Even her clothes don't fit me. They have developed baggy creases where the flesh is eroding from my bones.

The nights are another thing. I still can't sleep. My heart won't slow down enough for my brain to stop working. It is jammed in fight-or-flight mode. I lie awake replaying that conversation at the end of the blue bed, over and over, as if my mind is trying, belatedly, to warn me of the wave about to overtake me. Without sleep, though, I can't work and without work I can't get through this thing.

I visit a doctor, a young man whose desk is covered with photos of his wife and children. His face fills with something a bit like shame when I describe what has happened. He quickly gives me a prescription for some white pills that will pull me under and hold me down when I need them to.

I try to keep researching shyness, tracking down journal articles on social anxiety and the fear of rejection. Now more than ever I need to understand this thing and how it might be controlled.

I walk my sister's dog, or allow the dog to walk me, up and down the path beside the river, past the industrial warehouses converted into waterfront condominiums, past the Vietnamese fishermen squatting in silence on the old wooden jetties, under the railway bridges where neon graffiti defies the shadows. I stop to stare at a trail of starfish washed up on the riverbank, their pocked arms curling in the sun, and wonder what these creatures are doing so far from where they belong.

And I swim. I find an outdoor pool near my new home and every day I slide under that shimmering sheet of blue and let my fast-beating heart power me up and down, thirty long laps, staring through the wet blur inside my watertight goggles, trying again and again to make sense of that night. Through some strange alchemy of reverse deliquescence, the chlorinated water embraces my liquid body and my flesh becomes solid again. For about an hour after I haul myself out of the pool, calves cramping, I feel calmer. The day can be got through, just.

But then the fear returns and with it, the overwhelming sense that a part of me is missing.

> **Belonging:** to fit into, have a home, have a rightful place, to go with, be part of, related to, attach to, be connected with, have a proper place, be associated with, be included in, be allied to, be affiliated with, be an adherent of.

With Tom, I had belonged. And when we were apart I would be longing for him. But that was okay because I knew that we would be together for a long time. Not owning each other, not completing each other, just connecting, fitting together.

I can't make it make sense, and so I do what we have always done. Smothering my pride, I write to Tom, a long loving email suggesting he reconsider his decision. I remind him of all the pleasures there have been and there might yet be if we can just find a way through this strange mess. The next morning there is a short reply waiting for me in the inbox. He's sorry but he still feels the same way.

'All writers must first charm and then betray' says the quote stuck to the wall above my desk. I thought it was a metaphor. Perhaps I have been wrong about that too.

On Textual Intercourse

When Tom was working away from home he used to write to me every night. A letter from London. A missive from Massachusetts. A poem from Paris. Words were our love tokens. They kept the connection. They counted for a lot.

So when the actor Russell Crowe was being pilloried for throwing a phone across an American hotel lobby because he couldn't call his wife back home in Australia at precisely the time he had promised to call her, I surprised a few friends by defending him. 'Maybe she really needed him to make that call,' I said. 'Maybe the timing of that call counted for a lot.'

Some Questions You Might Ask Yourself at 3 a.m.

When Tom was away from home:

Did he sit down and write to me *before* he had chosen the other woman he would fuck that night? I guess that way he could feel like he had a clean slate. No sin had yet been committed, no shame could seep into the text. The coast was clear.

Did he sit down and write to me *after* he had chosen but *before* he had fucked the other woman? I guess that way he wouldn't have to worry about forgetting to write to me afterwards, or feeling too post-coitally sleepy to bother, or accidentally letting slip some detail in the email that might make me suspicious.

Did he sit down and write to me *after* he had chosen and *after* he had fucked the other woman? I guess that way he wouldn't have to risk any stray thoughts of me interrupting his manoeuvres. He could send her home and get back to his laptop.

Did he sit down and write to me *in between* fucking *different* women? I guess there's no reason he should have kept it to one a night. If the offers were there, I mean. What's the difference between one or several other women? Writing to me might have been a nice little break. A palate cleanser.

Did he think of those other women as hamburgers, or as steak? Or as some other variety of meat?

The Catalogue Aria

The white pills from the doctor give me a few hours' sleep each night. During the days, though, they make me want to lie down all the time. One evening Professional Sian drags me off the mattress on the floor of my sister's spare room and drives me to the theatre. I am there to review *Don Giovanni*, an opera about a man who brags he has had one thousand and three lovers—'mille e tre!'—in Spain alone. I need a drink before the show begins. My friend and I prop at the bar next to the theatre.

'So Tom has been spotted,' she announces. 'With another woman. Another blonde.'

Please don't tell me.

Tell me.

'They were at a restaurant and he was holding her hand.'

No don't tell me.

'She looks a bit like you, apparently, only younger.'

I flee to a toilet cubicle where breathing is almost impossible.

'I am true to you,' Tom had said.

'You make monogamy a good place to be.'

'There's no one else.'

Don't tug on a loose thread. Once the thread has been loosened, though, sometimes the whole thing will come apart of its own accord. Ten years of facts are unravelling, leaving only loose shreds of fiction.

'Who knows what's truth and what's fiction? And does it matter?' Tom had asked.

Yes. Yes it does.

One Last Mirror

A month after Tom ends our relationship I return to our home with a screwdriver. Knowing his habits, I wait until he will be out for the afternoon. A few twists for each screw and the mirror comes away from the wardrobe door. I hug the reflection of my headless torso as I carry the mirror out through the gate and lay it carefully on a blanket in the back of my car. Quietly closing the front door on The Living Museum of Me, I drive back to my sister's house.

Catoptrophobia means the fear of mirrors. Or, more accurately, fear of the reflections within the mirror itself.

I wonder if there's a different term to describe a fear of mirrors that you imagine might be reflecting someone else.

What I Wanted

I don't see Tom anymore. There are still emails, tedious negotiations over my need to collect bits of my stuff from the house we used to share. There are pseudo-polite letters between our lawyers. Our bodies remain apart.

Tom is famous, though, so he is often in the media. My sister advises me to stop reading the newspapers but I am a journalist. I have to keep up. So she tries to shield me by checking the arts pages before I read them. Every now and then the system fails. An image of Tom's face ambushes me from the dark forest of newsprint and my startled heart pounds away at my ribs, trying to escape.

In an article about the local film industry an excited reporter mentions that the documentary about Tom is nearly finished. Remembering the hymn of praise I offered up in my interview with the documentary-makers, my stomach turns over. I can hear posterity snickering. I send a brief email to one of the film's producers, asking for my interview not to be used. His response is all barely suppressed irritation: as a journalist, *surely* I should know how inconvenient that would be for the documentary-makers?

Clearly he has no idea what has happened.

I politely suggest he ask Tom why I might prefer my interview to stay on the cutting-room floor. The interview is duly dropped and I wonder briefly if, somewhere in the world, there is a special cemetery where all the tragi-comic, mistimed interviews-that-have-no-place-in-posterity are laid to rest.

I remember then that Tom and I used to have a running joke. Every time he took a photo of me, some part of my body would be missing. Half a head. An arm severed from a shoulder. Legs chopped off below the knees. His 'arty shots', we called them. 'You're trying to make me disappear, aren't you, one limb at a time,' I once suggested with a smile.

When the documentary about Tom is released my sister's protective strategy fails completely. He is ubiquitous. And like a ghost haunting her own wake, I can't resist reading some of the newspaper articles about the film. One writer expresses mild curiosity that, although Tom's two ex-wives were interviewed in the documentary, there is no footage, no mention at all, of his former girlfriend of ten years, Sian Prior.

I have become what I always wanted to be.

Or what I always *thought* I wanted to be.

Invisible me.

A Masked Ball

The trade union choir is having a twenty-first birthday party. I was hounding them earlier in the year, encouraging them to celebrate. At last they have decided to mark the milestone with a big old knees-up. They want me to host the event.

I can't do it. They will see through me, through my professional façade. See that I have changed from solid to liquid.

But if I say no to this, what other battles will I concede to my fear? And then what will be left of me? I have to hang on to the part of me that hasn't been dependent on Tom's regard.

So I put on a pink spotted party frock and go to the Trades Hall with my carefully written script and my even more carefully constructed party smile. Waiting in the foyer beforehand I practise my small talk with the comrades and avoid any questions about my private life. I hide my shaking glass of water under a seat and when the time comes I step up to the microphone and become Comrade Choir Mistress again. The fear-adrenaline that has been coursing through me for days is instantly converted into a fizzing performance high.

I tease, I praise, I flirt, I reminisce. I remind them about our first ever gig in a high wind under the West Gate Bridge, how helpless we all felt when the choir's four-part harmonies collapsed just as the bridge itself had collapsed two decades before. I joke about shaking Nelson Mandela's hand on stage at the Town Hall after we serenaded him with the ANC's anthem, and how I hadn't washed my hand since. I dole out generous dollops of *pos re,* describing my memories of recording our first collection of songs in a bluestone church where even the hard-line atheist comrades sang like angels.

At the end of the evening when the comrades are backslapping their way to the pub for a few rounds of nostalgia, I quietly slip away. The choir mistress persona has served me well but the fear still lies just under the surface. Better not push my luck.

Now that I have proven to myself that I can keep it together in public, I begin accepting other gigs, even seeking them out. I host a symphony concert, co-present a radio program, interview authors in front of a live audience. I take on more teaching. I even agree to sing in a theatre production to be performed in a festival in France. I just keep saying yes to anything that I think will test me.

Sometimes, though, even Professional Sian can't hold back the liquefaction.

I agree to help interview a batch of prospective writing students at the university. Sitting with a colleague in an airless fluorescent classroom, I try to maintain a reassuring smile as the candidates file in one by one to answer our questions about their reading and writing habits. I can see their top lips beading with sweat, their shoulders hunching with nerves. I can hear how self-consciousness is robbing them of the ends of their sentences, can tell how desperately they want this thing that we can offer or withhold, and how much they fear that we will reject them.

Somehow their distress begins to leak into mine, swelling my throat, blocking my lungs. When the door closes behind a girl whose handshake is slippery with sweat, I call a halt. 'My back is killing me,' I tell my colleague. 'I need to lie down for fifteen minutes or I won't get through the day.' It isn't exactly a lie. Over the past few weeks grief and overexercise have hardened my body into a knot of pain. But this is something different.

After my colleague has set off to find a cup of tea I lock the door and lower myself to the classroom floor. Looking along my supine body I register a series of small shocks. There are my feet, splayed at the end of my trembling legs. There are my hands, clasped tight over my churning belly. But are they really mine? It seems doubtful, because surely I have melted into the sticky carpet like a cartoon character. Scrabbling for the mobile phone I dial the number of my friend Nella.

'I can't manage this,' I whisper to her. 'I feel like I'm disappearing. What should I do?'

'Remember, it's not about *you*,' Nella says. 'It's about *him*. There's nothing wrong with you. Just keep telling yourself that. It's *not* about you.' The meaning of her words can't penetrate the fog but just the sound of her voice begins to open up my constricted lungs. It is a sound I first heard when we shared a house two decades ago, a sound that accompanied

- New Year's Eve dinners on a long dining table that we hauled across the road from our house to the local football oval
- consultations over the lending and borrowing of frayed op-shop treasures from our wardrobes
- sweaty garden bees where we hacked into the backyard jungle of our rental house like Victorian lady explorers

    – weeping sessions in the bathroom when one of us regretted
      dumping a boy we could never love enough.

Had those boys felt like this? Until now I had always been the one who withdrew, the dumper rather than the dumpee, never giving myself a chance to practise dealing with this kind of calamity.

I lie there taking shallow breaths while Nella talks and talks into my ear, reciting lists of people who care about me, talking me back into my body, until I can get up off the sticky floor and re-affix the professional smile to my face.

A Merry Christmas

In mid-December I catch a cold. The lump in my throat becomes a sore throat which becomes laryngitis and my voice disappears. Something else is happening to my nervous system. My entire body begins to feel slightly numb. It is as if I've had a massive dental anaesthetic that's spread from my face to my toes, then failed to recede when the drugs wore off.

Is this the extra layer of skin I craved? Or an invisible scarring of my epidermis to protect what's inside? If anything, I feel less protected. With the outer layer numb, it simply means the next layer feels more. My tastebuds join the strike and eating becomes even more of a chore. Some sensations remain, like heat and cold, and the fear still washes through me every hour or so like a scalding tide.

When my voice begins to re-emerge it is a hoarse, broken thing, like a weak radio signal coming and going. Entire syllables drop out of the middle of my words, forcing me to repeat myself like a perseverative child.

The week leading up to Christmas Day (the day for families,

for children, for the gathering of clans) is like sliding down the inside of a volcano. Below me is a spitting broth of loneliness and self-pity. There is nothing I can do to slow my descent. I try, though.

I write lists.

- Christmas presents to be bought (a shorter list this year, since my family circle has more than halved).

- Possessions to be retrieved from my former home the next time I can bear to go there (the lawn I used to mow is now almost knee-high).

- Houses for rent on the other side of town (clicking through images on cheery real estate websites, endless photos of rooms with all the lights on but nobody home).

- Things to pack for a walking trip to the mountains with Nella (comforting self-protective items like insect repellent, sunscreen, elastic bandages and vodka).

- A new file on my computer entitled *Consolations: Things I Will Be Glad To Do Without* from my relationship with Tom (surprisingly long and occasionally comforting, like swigging on a cough elixir).

- A list of the human qualities I value and can't allow to be swamped by my anger and fear—kindness, honesty, love, empathy, love, generosity, love, love, love.

On Christmas Eve there is no list that can prevent the slide towards the caldera. A brief email from Tom submerges me entirely. After all those fresh-minted words of passion he has written to me over the years, so carefully crafted to surprise and delight, now he sounds like a Hallmark card: *Thinking of you and your family for Christmas and wishing you well for the New Year.*

221

Sometimes banality can be the cruellest language of all.

That night I lie on the mattress on the floor of my sister's front room and allow the tears to overtake me, croaking and gulping like some strange amphibious reptile, soaking handkerchief after handkerchief. Pure liquefaction. There is no way back, and yet I can't see a way forward. Nothing can fill the hole left by the loss of that love, that fantasy of love.

I feel my sister kneeling beside me, smoothing my hair, kissing my forehead over and over, patting my shoulders and whispering, 'This will pass, I promise you, this *will* pass.'

When my sister leaves the room I stare at the small mountain of boxes lined up on the bedside table, different coloured sleeping pills from several different doctors. I stare at them for a long time.

Somehow the night passes and when I wake on Christmas morning the sun has come up. We sit on the carpet beside the gum tree branch that serves as a Christmas tree and exchange gifts. I find that by concentrating hard on my nephew's face as he tears at the wrapping paper I can keep my own face fixed in an indulgent smile. Fake it till you make it.

The swimming pools are all closed so I can't do my laps. I have made a list of small tasks to get me through the day, and stop me panicking.

- Vacuum the car.
- Wash the car.
- Polish the car.

When I run out of car things, my sister sees my glassy eyes and invents some new tasks to keep the fear at bay.

- Wash the dishes generated by Yoni's cooking frenzy.
- Set the dinner table for our family of ten (not eleven).

- Spoon creamed cheese onto slices of smoked salmon, and
  roll them up.

Outside the steamy weather develops its own momentum.
Huge black clouds roll over the western suburbs and hurl punish-
ing bolts of lightning at each other. As I lean over the kitchen
bench, tussling with the sticky pink flesh of the smoked fish, I
think of King Lear, incandescent with rage, shouting uselessly
at the thundering skies. Shouting for me and for all the rejected
self-pitying people who have ever trodden the earth. If my voice
was working properly I might have gone out into the garden and
stood under the crazy hailstones and done some shouting too.
But where was the dignity in croaking at clouds?

When the rest of the family arrives—Margot and John, my
brother David and his wife and daughters—I submerge myself in
the crazy-weather talk and the ritualised teasing, the gift-giving
and joke-telling and overeating. With every glass of champagne
the slow minutes speed up until I stop noticing them passing.

When the food has all been eaten and the rain and hail have
finally abated, and when my brother and my parents have gone
home, the rest of my old-new family and I go walking up the
street, merry-christmasing the neighbours who have come out
for some fresh air. At the local park the dog sniffs every tree
('checking her messages,' Yoni says) and I throw wide balls to my
patient nephew who hits them back to me with a yellow plastic
cricket bat. The black cumulus clouds have gone, replaced by a
symphony of pink and orange cirrus. And I am still here.

Self in Other

Surprising Things That Your Friends Might Do

Send you a letter in the mail containing a voucher for a massage with a thin Frenchwoman whose surprisingly muscular arms will bully the pain out of your body and leave you feeling temporarily weightless.

Invite you to their home and persuade you to climb onto the inflatable dinosaur in their swimming pool and take a photo of you laughing with surprise as you fall off it, just to prove to you that you can still laugh.

Take you hiking for a week up and down snow-capped mountains and distract you from your breathless grief with their surprising knowledge of linguistics terms, including 'Janus words'—words that can have completely opposite meanings—a term that makes you wonder if perhaps the word 'monogamous' could legitimately have opposite meanings for you and for Tom.

Encourage you to start playing multiple Words With Friends games with them, which offers surprisingly effective respite at three in the morning from the endless mental replays of your last night with Tom.

Send you long emails expressing how surprised—no, shocked—they are to hear that you and their old friend Tom are no longer together because they thought he had never before seemed as happy as he had since the two of you had been together.

Take you walking along the beach path in a bracing wind and listen to your interminable theme-and-variations about what had happened between you and Tom and refrain from telling you that perhaps it wasn't entirely surprising that a man who had already left two wives might have gone on to leave his long term girlfriend.

Take you to a twilight concert at the zoo and let you lie on their picnic rug and weep behind your sunglasses while they dance to the sound of lions roaring with rage at the sound of humans playing intolerably loud rock'n'roll.

Invite you to the beach and accompany you into the surf, even if it's thirteen degrees Celsius and raining hard, because they know only the surf can pummel your grief into submission.

A Different Poison

Not long after I first start sleeping in my sister's spare room Margot is laid low by a series of headaches. Her headaches turn into migraines, a cavalcade of them colonising her skull, leaving her reeling with pain and nausea. She takes to wearing earplugs and sunglasses day and night to try to shut out the assailing world. Nothing the doctor prescribes makes any difference. Each time I see her she seems to have shrunk a little more. I ask my friends who suffer from the same affliction about causes, treatments, cures, snake oils, but nothing helps.

Eventually Margot's symptoms become so acute John has to take her to hospital. There she is hooked up to a drip of painkillers and anti-nausea drugs. 'We need to break the cycle,' the doctors tell us. It is the same hospital where my brother David, a cardiologist, is working. He comes straight down from his office and meets us in the ward, where the three of us hover anxiously beside Margot's bed, tugging the thin cotton blankets over her cold feet. Seeing her lying there with her eyes closed, her skin grey and her mouth slightly open, for the first time I can picture what my mother might look like inside a coffin. The snaking fear in my belly coils even tighter. I can't lose anything more.

The doctors eventually send Margot home again and the search for the right migraine pills goes on. There is a steady flow of emails between my siblings, our aunts and Margot's friends, all of us fretting about how helpless we feel. In one of those emails an old friend of Margot's hints to me that she thinks there might be a link between my current misery and my mother's illness, and that when I start feeling better, perhaps Margot will too.

I stare at the computer screen, reading those words over and over. There has always been an empathy feedback loop between Margot and me. At times each of us has tried to hide her unhappiness to avoid causing the other distress. Sometimes the feedback loop is a three-way thing that includes Yoni. We all spend a lot of time worrying about whether the other two are okay. These last few months, though, I haven't had the wherewithal to hide anything, not from my family. They are my refuge. Has my liquid terror somehow leaked into my mother's brain and poisoned it?

If so, I have another good reason to find a way to get on top of this thing. Time to break the cycle. I grit my teeth, email Tom (who is away travelling, yet again) and make arrangements to visit my former home one last time. I will pack my life into cardboard boxes and put it into storage until I can find somewhere else to live. A clean break is required: a full stop. Or at least a semi-colon.

Air of Yesterday

There is one cardboard box I can't leave in the storage
warehouse. *What if* there is a flood or a fire? *What if* the heavens
crack open again and a rogue lightning bolt takes out the big
metal container where my possessions are stacked to the roof?
On the long dusty day I spend dismantling the Living Museum
of Me, I carefully pack a box of treasures that I can't think of
losing and take it home to Yoni's: letters, photos, diaries, several
crumbling music scores that belonged to my grandparents, and
some fragments of my father's life.

- A green *Musician's Union Diary,* no bigger than the palm
  of my hand, from the year 1964
- A Cambridge *Holy Bible,* not much bigger than the diary
  with a zip-up leather binding and the letters *G.C.P.* printed
  in gold on the front
- A Baby Brownie camera, a little box of hard plastic and
  corroded silver
- A silver metal compass with a dented casing and a wobbling
  blue arrow

- A leather motorcycle cap, its fur lining moth-eaten and falling apart
- An empty brown leather glasses case labelled *Optical Prescription—Spectacle Makers Pty Ltd.*
- A collection of black and white photographs, the smallest passport-sized, the largest framed behind glass
- A hardback children's picture book that has begun to warp in the middle

A few weeks after I lock the gate at Tom's home for the last time, I haul the box of treasures out from where I've stashed it behind the couch in Yoni's spare room. Opening the plastic bag containing the collection of Glen's things, I begin pulling them out one by one.

The black binding of the picture book is fading to grey but the title still stands out in bold silver lettering: THE BOOK OF SPLENDID 'PLANES. Even if it hadn't been in such a worn condition, the book's title would give away its age. It has been many decades since anyone bothered putting an apostrophe in front of the word 'planes'. And 'splendid' disappeared from the Australian vernacular about the same time as 'rum cove'. I open a page at random.

A sheep and a cockerel are standing rigid, facing in opposite directions, and a duck is peering out from between the sheep's front legs. Above their heads hangs the moon-like orb of a hot-air balloon. Behind them a snow-capped mountain rises in the distance. The animals look so surprised to find themselves in Monsieur Montgolfier's new flying machine.

The image has been reproduced from an old engraving and the heading reads *The Air of Yesterday*. A woman squats in the foreground of the picture, her hands hanging loose and empty, her bonnet-framed face lifted to the skies in wonderment. Above the picture on the opposite page it reads *The Descent of the Air Balloon* and by the look of it they have had a crash landing. In the foreground, the squatting woman now tumbles on the grass, bonnet askew, feet waving in the air. Oh foolish, frightened woman.

I find myself wondering whether there is a connection between the masculine derring-do depicted in *The Book of Splendid 'Planes* and the story I had heard of teenage Glen canoeing down the main street of his home town when a sudden flood turned it into a river. Or the story of his death. A shy man who had pushed himself out into the world. A physical risk-taker.

I've had this picture book for many years, stored with other treasured objects—love letters from Andre, a fragment of pink coral, a piece of the Berlin Wall—in a polished wooden box that my stepfather John made for me when I was a teenager. I can't remember when the book came to me or how, but I've been keeping its existence quiet in case one of my siblings tries to 'borrow' it. Ever since my brother claimed ownership of our father's leather motorcycle jacket not long after I started wearing it to university, I have said nothing about my small collection of Glen's possessions. Perhaps my siblings have been doing the same with theirs.

On the first page of *The Book of Splendid 'Planes* there is an inscription written in my grandmother Mavis's elegant cursive: 'For Glenthorne Cadle Prior, Xmas 1943'. He would have been about nine years old. Turning over the yellowing pages, staring at the black and white photos of leather-helmeted men in their magnificent flying machines, I realise that this is the first time I have ever looked closely at the book. It has moved with me from house to house, relationship to relationship, and I have occasionally referred to it nostalgically in conversations with friends. In an abstract way, I have always liked the idea that my hands could touch something that Glen's touched. In all this time, though, I have never actually read it cover to cover.

Why have I had so little curiosity about this man until recently? He has been a cardboard cut-out father, propped in the wings, waiting for the appropriate cue in the melodrama of my life before he can be dragged out into the light. Or a sentimental treat, perhaps, stored up for a rainy day when I am feeling wistful and want to prolong the feeling. Now I feel wistful for the days when wistfulness seemed like a potentially enjoyable emotional state.

Next I open the green diary from 1964. On the first page is printed a list of the names of the National Executive Committee of the Musicians Union of Great Britain. At the beginning of that year Margot and Glen were still living in London, playing in orchestras together. *Arise ye workers from your slumbers* with your galloping French horns and your rumbling bass clarinets and your angelic harps. So my trumpet-playing father was a union comrade too. Good on him.

Most of the entries in Glen's writing seem to be about rehearsals and performances. Messy handwriting. Drunken ant-trails, like mine. Lists of times and initials, shorthand, minimal. No clues there. Some time in the first half of the year I know my parents returned to Australia by boat, Margot retching her way across the oceans with a combination of morning sickness and seasickness.

The date of my birth, 22 August, has two scribbled entries for performances, one at 2 p.m. and one at 8 p.m., and judging from the number of scrawls in the following pages, the week after I was born was the busiest of the whole year for Glen. Poor Margot.

I flip forward to 18 November. It was a Wednesday. There is something written in pencil there, a full sentence rather than the usual lists. I can't decipher it. *Green something something park up the something something.* I stare and stare at those words, holding them up to the light, trying to make sense of the sentence. Wednesday. What were the orchestra comrades doing, having a picnic at the beach on a Wednesday?

The hand-written entries continue, at least for a while. More times and initials, more rehearsals planned, even a reference to a birthday party Yoni was to go to a couple of weeks later. All the way up to 19 December 1964, when the diary tells me Glen was due to play in a performance of Handel's *Messiah*. Why am I so surprised? Diaries are for planning ahead. Did I think the pages would go blank from that day in November just because he had stopped breathing?

Handel loved the trumpet. He must have. So many exquisite solos and duets for sweet, high brass. How many times over the years have I listened to the *Messiah*, this hymn of praise to a man who so many believe will never die? I wonder who played Glen's parts in the orchestra that night in December 1964 and whether they knew they were playing in the place of a dead man.

Black and White

A studio photo of Glen in profile, blond short back and sides struggling against the Brylcreem; wearing a suit and tie, holding his trumpet to his mouth. Hands slightly blurry from movement, as if he really was playing, not just posing for the picture. One elbow leaning on a raised knee, those long legs covered in baggy pants. Glasses hiding his eyes, staring straight ahead, avoiding the camera's gaze. Face unlined, my nose, my chin. Black suit, white background. Chiaroscuro Dad.

A black and white photo of Margot and Glen standing on a city street. Holding hands. He is a head taller than her and they are leaning in towards each other, their torsos pulled together by an invisible force, like Stan Prior's magnets. She is wearing a pale cardigan and smiling into the camera. He is in a thick roll-neck jumper but he's not smiling. Serious Dad.

A newspaper clipping of Glen holding five-year-old Yoni in his arms, smiling so broadly the whole shape of his face has changed, disintegrated. Mine does that too when I smile. The doting father, home from a country tour with the state symphony orchestra. Happy Dad.

A torn black and white photo of Glen leaning forward, eyebrows raised, pretending to sip tea from a thimble-sized teacup, the tiny toy saucer held carefully in his long fingers. Nutty Dad.

A photo of a group of musicians on a stage, girls in cardigans dancing together in the foreground, a curtain festooned with balloons in the background, an upright piano against the wall, and in the back line of the band a blond head with glasses, a trumpeter. Jazz Dad.

On the last page of *The Book of Splendid 'Planes* there is another black and white photo. A boy wearing shorts, long socks and a black cap has climbed a tree. He is staring away from the camera, holding on to a dead branch and leaning back into the sky. Above his cap a dozen planes are frozen in a perfect V formation at the edge of the picture. Behind the tree in the distance is a bank of clouds and, by chance or by artifice, the boy looks like he is standing on a thick cushion of cumulus. Beside the photo is printed one word: "Goodbye."

Fact versus Fiction

When my best friend Sally turned nine she invited all of her best friends to the movies. For her birthday outing she chose *The Poseidon Adventure*. When the wave hit and the ship turned upside down I paused mid-Fantale and clung on tight to the leather elbow rests beside my seat. One by one the characters were picked off by the screenwriters, a different gruesome end for each of them, and at the end of the movie the survivors climbed, blinking, out into the glaring light that poured down on the bottom of the capsized ship. As the theme song played—'there's got be a morning after'—we all followed Sally, blinking, out into the glare of the cinema foyer.

I couldn't speak.

For months after Sally's birthday my nightmares were filled with burning bodies and mass drownings and waves that lurched up out of nowhere and swept me away. They still are.

Six months after the night I packed a suitcase and drove to Yoni's house, I move out again and into my new home. The suburb where I lived with Tom now feels like a radiation exclusion zone for me. I have found a place across the river, on the other side of town. I throw a house-warming party, inviting all my friends and many of Tom's relations, and give a speech. There is a long list (of course) of all the people to be thanked. I describe myself as a ship that has gone aground and tell them they have hauled me to safety. I reassure them I am safe now and they don't need to worry about me anymore. That is almost true and they seem happy to hear it. I drink more than three glasses of wine and don't mind that most of my friends are too busy talking to each other to bother dancing. Talking is good. Silence has never suited me.

After I unpack all the cardboard boxes and set up my new home office, I plug my father's name into an internet search engine. This is the second time I have tried googling Glen and, once again, three entries come up.

The first entry takes me to a list of the participants in National Music Camp, 1952, including *Glenthorne Prior—Cornet*. There are other names on the list that I recognise: the first husband of my clarinet teacher; a trombonist who taught my stepbrother to play; a double-bass player who was a close friend of my father's. Names that conjure the smells of cork grease and bamboo reeds, of saliva dripping from tarnished brass bells, of rosin and lip balm and teenage sweat and dusty sheet music. How many of these people are still alive, I wonder, and of those, how many would remember Glen? What stories could they recall about him now and how many of them would be true?

The double-bass player played in jazz bands with Glen, and he and Margot remained friends after my father's death. I remember he once described how my father had struggled with the musical freedom of jazz, saying that Glen wasn't 'loose enough to let it swing'. It is a phrase that has sometimes snuck into my head when I have been feeling rigid with shyness.

The second Google hit takes me through to a website called 'Find A Grave'. Glen's name sits there quietly in the middle of the screen while pop-up ads for fee-free bank accounts and video software flash around it.

The third item on the Google list is a website address: *Listphile.com*

A website for lovers of lists. I click through, hoping there might have been a change since the last time I looked. But no—the same words appear.

World Shark Attack Database: Fatal Shark Attack, Prior.

Description
Glenthorne Prior age 29 was fatally attacked on November 18th, 1964 while swimming to rescue swimmers in trouble out at Fingal Beach, near Tweed Heads. *Daily Mirror (Sydney), 11/19/1964 edition*

Date of Attack
November 18, 1964

Type of Shark
Unknown

Survive
No

Hands poised over the keyboard, my fingers begin to tingle with a familiar blood-rush. Not true. There was no shark. He drowned. They found his body, eventually. Washed up, days later, further down the coast. Intact, as far as I know.

There was no shark.

Someone made that up. Someone on the *Daily Mirror* (a journalist maybe, someone like me) decided the story of a father of three who drowned saving the lives of two young people while his wife watched from the shore wasn't an interesting enough story. So they added a shark for dramatic impact. Then someone took that story and added it to their list of shark stories and now Google was spreading the lies.

There was no shark.

Why am I so angry? Because someone else has been careless with the truth?

'You make monogamy a good place to be.' And: 'I am true to you.' Perhaps, in his mind, what Tom said was a version of the truth. A story he told himself until he was overtaken by 'the pretendies' and had to stop.

Tom has just recorded a new collection of songs about a relationship break-up. In one of Tom's songs the man desperately wants to sleep with someone new, but decides he won't because he still loves the woman he's with. Later in the narrative, the woman leaves the man anyway.

A sympathetic female listener might fall a little bit in love with the man who is left by the one he remains faithful to. Or even with that man's creator—if, as we all do, she mistakes fiction for facts.

Sometimes the truth slips away between the gaps in the stories we tell about ourselves. Sometimes we push it through the gaps ourselves so we can make better stories. Reshape the characters. Make them more interesting, more heroic, more lovable. More deserving of sympathy. Less likely to be rejected.

About the Sea

I have been asked to perform an Australian song cycle in an art gallery. *Sea Chronicles* is written for soprano and string quartet, and the third song is based on a poem called 'Life Saver'. In this song I have to sing the words

> *He is drowned, the tall one.*
> *Thin brother Death has him by the throat*
> *On the sand, in the sun.*

Learning this song cycle is proving to be quite difficult. A familiar lump swells in my throat every time I try to practise, getting in the way of the music. But it will be okay on the day, I tell myself. Professional Sian will see to that.

One morning as I'm eating breakfast in my new kitchen a report comes on the radio about a mathematician who is trying to find a formula to measure the relative danger of waves on surf beaches. It's for safety reasons, the mathematician says. To prevent drownings.

We humans are so optimistic. We persuade ourselves that if we can find a way to quantify things, or to understand exactly how they work, we can control them. Or at least control their effects. That's why I first started writing this story: to get on top of my shyness.

What if Glen could have mathematically predicted the danger of the waves at that surf beach? Would he have stopped himself entering the water? Would he *not* have tried to save those people from drowning?

What if I had thought for a moment about the simple mathematics of Tom's past relationships: twice married, twice divorced, both times after *he* left her? Would I have tried to stop myself falling in love with him?

What if there was a mathematical formula that could prove to us that for every moment, every hour, every year of intense happiness we experience in our lives, we will experience an equally intense period of misery? Would we try to avoid happiness?

Brahms' Clarinet Sonata

There on the shining timber stage of the recital hall is a black music stand all spiked and waiting. Waiting for the dapper man with the ripple of silver keys in his hands to lick the sliver of bamboo and flex his elbows.

As if by magic he begins playing at precisely the same millisecond the pianist begins playing and suddenly the spike and the dapperness are gone and it's all heart.

It's all honeyed phrases spiralling into the hall and through your body and into the past when you knew these phrases better than you've known any music since, phrases that took hours of mingled pleasure and resentment as you bit down on the reed and ignored the sunny afternoon outside so you could make the honey flow.

Back then there were the Saturday morning clarinet lessons and the teacher with the chic bob who stood beside you singing the honeyed phrases and telling you about the sadness of Brahms and about this, one of the last chamber pieces Brahms ever composed, at the exhausted end of the Romantic era. The last flare of music from the saddest of men in that era of mannered sadness.

Telling you about Brahms and his sadness, willing you to understand and to make the understanding into honey, and part of you knew what she meant, but most of you didn't really know, and that unknowing part knew that you would have to wait, that you would only truly know when you'd had the sadness too.

And there on the shining timber stage, just behind the dapper swaying clarinettist, sits an invisible man, a ghost man, a man called Tom who just one night ago in this very same hall breathed this very same air and sang his ghost songs to a crowd just like this one. Except you weren't there. You'll never be there. Not anymore.

And as the clarinet sings the sadness of Brahms into that air, you remember the last time you played this music to an audience, just the three of them, seated in a row behind a long table, heads down, scribbling into their notebooks just as you're scribbling in this notebook now.

Three decades ago you played them the honey and when you had finished the audience of examiners looked up and smiled their widest smiles and said—What next?

You turned the page to the next piece, another sonata, and nodded to your pianist. And just as you were about to play, one of the three audience members held up her hand and said—No. You can't. Not this one. It's not on the syllabus.

And all the lonely sunny afternoons spent in front of the spiky music stand suddenly froze into One Big Mistake. It's the wrong music.

It's the best, most brilliant, most difficult music you've ever learned. It's music that would make this audience of three sit back in their chairs and stare in wonder. But it's the wrong music. Not this one. You can't.

And was it in that moment that you decided? Was it in front of the spiky music stand three decades ago that you first knew there was a choice?

That you could make a big mistake, and you could give in to the fear and the sadness, and you could give up.

Or you could put down your clarinet, walk out into the hallway where all the other trembling clarinettists were sucking on their bamboo reeds and waiting to take their turn in front of the examiners. You could go up to each of those clarinettists and ask—What music do you have?

That you could grab something that looked playable and walk back into the room and pick up your clarinet and sight-read the fucker, note perfect, so that the audience of three sat back in their chairs and stared in wonder.

That you could beat the fear and the sadness.

And as the dapper clarinettist flexes and sways there on the timber stage through the final movement of the Brahms sonata, the ghost man fades from view. The man who gave up on the conversation with you, who taught you the most about the fear and the sadness, a lesson that can never be unlearned, that man is truly nothing more than a ghost now.

The dapper clarinettist plays the last phrase and the silence becomes the honey. And you look up from scribbling in your notebook, put down your pen, sit back in your chair and stare in wonder.

The Final Interview

I'm afraid my research has revealed some gaps in your story. You call this 'non-fiction' but there are some omissions and exaggerations, aren't there?

(Blushes) You're right. I have left things out. Of course, it would have been extremely tedious to put everything in. What do you want to know?

Let's begin with the end of your radio career. You told us how much you loved being a presenter, and then later you told us all about the print articles you were writing, but what happened in between? Why did a radio host suddenly become a newspaper columnist?

(Pauses) I got sacked. They don't call it that, they call it a 'non-renewal of contract', but effectively you've been sacked. I still don't know why. The reason I was given was that my program wasn't rating well enough. The boss had just been reassuring me that as long as the ratings were climbing steadily

(they were) my position was safe. Then suddenly he changed his mind and I was out. Some of my friends favoured a conspiracy theory: too many strong opinions on too many awkward topics, too openly expressed. Personally I doubt it. Deep down, I've always wondered if someone 'upstairs' at the radio station could hear my whispering *what if*s. Maybe someone saw through the 'illusion of competence' and decided that Shy Sian couldn't carry it off. Losing that job was the biggest rejection I had ever encountered. It nearly sank me. It certainly helped to sink the relationship I was in at the time. I was in love with radio and radio no longer wanted me. It was my first, maybe my only, rehearsal for dealing with Tom's rejection. One minute you're in favour, the next minute you're not. Baffling.

I'm sorry to have taken you back to such a painful episode. Here, have a glass of water. Now: you implied that Tom's rejection came as a complete shock to you but surely there must have been signs before that night? You had recently been overseas together having a holiday by the sea. What happened on that trip?

(Pauses again, longer this time) There was a small earthquake. I was in the shower. Open-air shower. Frangipani flowers hanging above my head. Feet covered with shampoo suds. Cold tap on for the sunburn. The door of the bathroom was open and I could see, through the bedroom window, dozens of tiny fishing boats skimming across the sea, on their way home. I wanted to be on one of them. When I came out of the bathroom Tom was lying on the bed reading. His feet looked so beautiful there on the white sheets. He said, 'I wonder if we should be worried.'

'About what?' I replied.

'About the earthquake.'

'What earthquake?' I said.

'The one that just happened!'

But I hadn't felt it. I had no idea. If he could feel it, why hadn't I felt it?

There's another omission I need to ask you about. You tell us Tom is famous, so everyone is probably wondering who he is, but you don't tell us his real name. Why so coy?

Because if you write a story that happens to have a famous person in it, everyone thinks you've written a story about a famous person. This isn't a story about Tom. This is a story about you and me and shyness. Anyone can find out who Tom is if they want to, but I'm hoping they'll read the book first and realise that although every famous person is different, fame itself doesn't change much. It always attracts the same kind of prurient and obsessive behaviour. It always draws attention towards itself and away from everything else. It makes potentially more interesting things fade into invisibility. And fame can make the famous feel like gods. Perhaps it's inevitable. All that relentless positive reinforcement. Toxic.

Did you think Tom could rescue you?

What do you mean?

You said earlier that you were in a well and he sent down a rope ladder. Had you been waiting all along for some handsome prince to rescue you from your shyness? And if so, how does that fit with your views about women and the disempowering effect of the Male Gaze? It's Feminism 101, surely, that women don't need the prince's kiss to deliver them agency?

Yes, well...

Speaking of rescuing, I can't help wondering what impact the manner of our father's death might have on all this. The man who died rescuing people. *Other* people, not you. The hero who disappeared from view. The unreachable, unattainable male.

I don't know. I'm an amateur with this stuff. Which I guess makes you one too. You're just better at bluffing. I don't know why, after all those years of being relatively uninterested in him, now just thinking about Glen undoes me. Maybe I've been hanging around on surf beaches my whole life waiting for him to appear. Waiting for a cold wet hug from a guy who was never loose enough to let it swing. Waiting for someone who knew me because I was just like him. Someone who loved me because he had to, because it was biologically predetermined, like our shyness.

But what about Tom?

I usually felt less shy when I was with him. Something about being bathed in his positive regard. Tom is a man who once said to me, 'I like who I am when I'm with you.' Maybe, like you and me, there were always several different versions of him and one of them was always going to leave me. While Tom and I were emailing each other during those first six months, I constructed a version of him based on what he wrote to me and what I'd read of his published writing, a version that fitted what Shy Sian needed. I thought what we had was romantic love. I thought we were a poem. In the end, though, we were just a string of platitudes.

(Silence)

The other day I heard an anthropologist on the radio saying that what we call romantic love is nothing more than a 'longing for association'. The social scientists always strip the poetry away, don't they? If they're right about that, you could say that I longed for someone like Tom so I imagined him into being. He was always a fantasy figure. So often silent. So often absent. If we're going to continue this amateur psychologising, I'd say that I projected onto him a whole lot of qualities he never had. Filled in the gaps with whatever suited me.

There's something more I need to say about love. You're not going to like this. It will make you squirm. The object of my love may have been imaginary but the love was real. It was the strongest thing I'd ever felt, stronger than my shyness. No wonder I didn't want to let it go.

(Not squirming but sceptical) How *can* you be in love with someone for ten years who was only ever 'imaginary', as you put it?

Because any evidence that didn't fit my fantasy was immediately dismissed. The version of Tom that I fell in love with had been crafted in text long before the first time we kissed. But our textual versions of ourselves can only ever be partial versions of ourselves—personas—just like you and me. And everything that happened after we met, I sculpted and reshaped to fit the imaginary version. When Tom was cool or dismissive with me, when he flirted with other women in my presence, when he lied to me about fucking those other women, I edited out the evidence that didn't fit with my fantasy. Because that perfect, imaginary version of him was my safety zone, the place where I believed I was accepted and loved for who I was, in spite of this shy disfigurement.

You remember how sometimes I confided in Margot about how difficult I found it dealing with Tom's frequent long absences, and with the way he always put work before everything else?

And how she once told me, 'He's just like your father; Glen's work always came first: it's a kind of deep selfishness'? I didn't want to hear those words. I edited them out too. I didn't want anything to topple the giant heroic statues I had made of both those men. But I never really knew Tom. I imagined a depth of intimacy that didn't exist, a strength of loyalty that was never there, a level of respect that was impossible. Margot knew Tom would leave me. She had even set aside some money to help me out when (not if) it happened. There's no way she could have warned me, though, is there?

No way at all. But she's pretty smart, our mother. Interesting, how you used the word 'disfigurement' to describe your shyness. There's a psychological condition I've been reading about called 'body identity integrity disorder'. People with this condition sometimes try to hack off one of their own perfectly normal, functioning limbs because they are convinced that limb doesn't belong to them. They believe it's an interloper and quite possibly dangerous to them. Perhaps shyness has been like that for you. It's a perfectly normal, natural part of your identity that you've been unable to acknowledge belongs to you, and you've been trying to remove it for decades.

That's a good theory.

So maybe you can give that up now, that self-mutilation thing? And while you're at it, you could also give up that looking-for-a-shortcut thing with dangerous imaginary men. Sorry, I don't mean to turn this into a counselling session, but ever since I can remember you've been sandwiched between these two fears—fear of people and fear of loneliness. *Leave me alone, don't leave me.* Maybe you can stop waiting to be rescued and try a bit of solitude for a change. It won't kill you, you know.

I overheard a conversation on a train recently. There was a woman sitting in front of me talking to her friend on a mobile—practically everyone on that train was doing something with their phones—and at one point she said to him, 'So what is your strategy for feeling safe with other people?' It sounded like a good question to me. I wrote it down—in my phone. Then I thought about it some more. Maybe what we need is not just a strategy for how to feel safe with other people, but for how to feel safe *without* other people. We're so afraid of loneliness. Sometimes the fantasy of romantic love can offer us respite, or a voice on the radio. But it's always there, waiting for us, looking back at us from the mirror when all we can see is a reflection of ourselves, alone.

I have one last question for you. Why are you so down on helpfulness? Maybe it's not such a bad thing.

I do like to help. It's nature *and* nurture. It's in the genes and it's been modelled for me by most of my elders, just like shyness. And it's too late, isn't it? I can't get rid of either of them. Shyness belongs to me; I am affiliated with it. And I'm still a compulsive improver.

That old list of ours, Things Wrong With The World, hasn't exactly shrunk in the last couple of decades. The world could still do with some improvement. In spite of your reservations, maybe this *could* be a self-help book after all, for other shy people. But you and I could give ourselves a break now and put that helpfulness energy elsewhere, instead of focusing it on ourselves. I'm a bit sick of us. In fact, here's an idea. Maybe we could stop thinking of ourselves as two separate personas, at least one of whom is in constant need of improvement, and get together. You and I could just be me.

Or me. Sure. It's worth a try. *(Pause)* You remember our grandmother Peg on the tandem bicycle with her octogenarian boyfriend?

Of course.

So. *(Pause)* You know we'll probably do it again, don't you?

What?

That 'longing for association' thing.

(Silence)   *(Smiles indulgently)*

READING LIST

Chen, X. (2010). Shyness-inhibition in childhood and adolescence: a cross-cultural perspective. *The Development of Shyness and Social Withdrawal*. New York, The Guildford Press: 213–35.

Coupland, J. (2001). *Small Talk*. London, Pearson PTR Interactive.

Darwin, C. (1872). *The Expression of the Emotions in Man and Animal*. London, John Murray.

Dunbar, R. (1996). *Grooming, Gossip and the Evolution of Language*. London, Faber and Faber.

Fine, D. (2005). *The Fine Art of Small Talk*. New York, Hyperion.

Goffman, E. (1959). *The Presentation of the Self in Everyday Life*. Middlesex, England, Penguin Books.

Goleman, D. (1996). *Emotional Intelligence: why it can matter more than IQ*. Bloomsbury.

Gorris, S. B. a. L. (2009). 'We Like Lists Because We Don't Want to Die'. *Spiegel Online*.

Hawley, J. (2011). 'The Quiet Achiever'. *Age*. Melbourne, Fairfax.

I Think They Think: Overcoming Social Phobia (1998). M. S. Productions.

Lane, C. (2007). *Shyness: How Normal Behaviour Became a Sickness*. London and New Haven, Yale University Press.

Little, G. (1985). *Political Ensembles*. Oxford, Oxford University Press.

Ogden, L. E. (2013). 'Survival of the Shyest'. *New Scientist*: 4.

Paley, V. G. (1992). *You Can't Say You Can't Play*. Cambridge, Massachusetts, Harvard University Press.

Probyn, E. (2005). *Blush: Faces of Shame*. Sydney, UNSW Press.

Saunders, P. and A. Chester (2008). 'Shyness and the internet: social problem or panacea?' *Computers in Human Behaviour* 24: 2649.

Scott, S. (2007). *Shyness and Society: the Illusion of Competence*. New York, Palgrave Macmillan.

Whitty, M. and A. Carr (2006). *Cyberspace Romance: The Psychology of Online Relationships*. Palgrave Macmillan.

ACKNOWLEDGMENTS

Heartfelt thanks:

For friendship, advice, loyalty, love: LD, ER, KM, SA, DJ, Jennifer H, Kathleen H, Karen V, Fiona P, Kate J, (the late) Deborah C, Mike K, Nola W, Peter C, Caroline L, Bagryana P, Robyn V, Sally N, Suzy Z, Di W-M, Melinda D, Andrea M, Nicki S, Sophie C, Steven B, John C, Reuben C, Julia P, Eloise P, Isabel P, Anne K, Mary-Jo K, Sheila K, Lynn K, Rebecca L, Alex M, Nellie M, Steve H and Deborah R.

For invaluable professional advice and support: Mandy Brett, Michael Heyward, Jane Novak, Jenny Darling, Aviva Tuffield, David Carlin, Brian Morris, Francesca Rendle-Short, Andrea Chester, Craig Batty, Clare Renner, Penny Johnson.

For the Readings Glenfern Fellowship: Iola Matthews, Mark Rubbo, Writers Victoria.

For sharing your stories: Sally S, Kate H, Jon F and my RMIT students and colleagues past and present.

For your courage and generosity in allowing me to tell my version of our story, and for your love: Margot, John, Yoni and David.

Some names have been changed to protect the privacy of individuals referred to in this memoir.

PUBLICATION ACKNOWLEDGMENTS

An early version of the hospital story: *Age* 'A2'

Essay: 'To my turning point' in *Women of Letters*, 2011, Penguin, Camberwell, pp. 368–74

Essay: 'Shaving the way to success' in *Focus on Writing*, 1987, Martin Educational in association with Robert Anderson and Associates, Hawthron, pp 14–15

Essay: 'Shy Young Thing' in *Meanjin*, 2009 68(2): pp. 58–66
http://meanjin.com.au/editions/volume-68-number-2-2009/article/shy-young-thing/

Radio essay: 'Shy Young Thing' broadcast Wednesday 21 July 2010, 10:40 a.m. on ABC Radio National 'First Person'
http://www.abc.net.au/radionational/programs/firstperson/shy-young-thing/3031334

Essay: 'Shy Young Thing' in *Rex Journal*, 2012, QUT Creative Writing and Literary Studies, Creative Industries Faculty, pp. 60–5